PARTICIPANT OBSERVATION

Applied Social Research Methods Series
Volume 15

Applied Social Research Methods Series

Series Editor:
LEONARD BICKMAN, Peabody College, Vanderbilt University
Series Associate Editor:
DEBRA ROG, National Institute of Mental Health

This series is designed to provide students and practicing professionals in the social sciences with relatively inexpensive softcover textbooks describing the major methods used in applied social research. Each text introduces the reader to the state of the art of that particular method and follows step-by-step procedures in its explanation. Each author describes the theory underlying the method to help the student understand the reasons for undertaking certain tasks. Current research is used to support the author's approach.

Volumes in this series:

PARTICIPANT OBSERVATION

A Methodology for Human Studies

Danny L. Jorgensen

Applied Social Research Methods Series
Volume 15

 SAGE PUBLICATIONS
The Publishers of Professional Social Science
Newbury Park   London   New Delhi

For information address:

SAGE Publications, Inc.
2111 West Hillcrest Drive
Newbury Park, California 91320

SAGE Publications Ltd.
28 Banner Street
London EC1Y 8QE
England

SAGE Publications India Pvt. Ltd.
M-32 Market
Greater Kailash I
New Delhi 110 048 India

Printed in the United States of America

Library of Congress Cataloging-in-Publication Data

Jorgensen, Danny L.
    Participant observation.

    (Applied social research methods series ; v. 15)
    Bibliography: p.
    Includes index.
    1. Participant observation. 2. Social sciences—
Field work. 3. Social sciences—Research—Methodology.
I. Title. II. Series.
H62.J625 1989 : 300'.72   88-26510
ISBN 0-8039-2876-9
ISBN 0-8039-2877-7 (pbk.)

FIRST PRINTING 1989

CONTENTS

PREFACE

This book provides an introduction to basic principles and strategies of *participant observation*. It is intended for students, professionals, academics, and scholars without previous background or experience with this methodology. Using the materials contained in this book, you can begin conducting participant observational research. This is an invitation to become familiar with and practice the unique methodology of participant observation.

There are several different conceptions of participant observation. From a *positivistic* standpoint—the view that human studies must conform to the methodology of the physical sciences, such as physics—participant observation sometimes is regarded as nonscientific (Easthope, 1971). More commonly, however, it is viewed positivistically as useful during the preliminary stages of scientific inquiry for exploration and description (Lazarsfeld, 1972; Babbie, 1986). Qualitative descriptions generated by participant observation are used to formulate concepts for measurement, as well as generalizations and hypotheses that with further testing may be used to construct explanatory theories. In short, then, from a positivistic viewpoint, participant observation is simply a special form of observation, a unique method of collecting data, but not otherwise useful for the ultimate scientific goal of explanatory theorizing.

More ardent advocates of this methodology sometimes have accepted this limited conception of participant observation as a method of data collection, or otherwise attempted to reconcile participant observation with a positivistic conception of human studies. Participant observation, for instance, has been seen as useful for measuring concepts, testing hypotheses, and/or constructing causal explanations (see McCall, 1978; Lofland and Lofland, 1984). More generally, however, participant observation has been conceptualized as fundamentally different from the methodology of the physical sciences, as a special methodology, uniquely adapted to the distinctive character of human existence. Though no less "scientific" than other research methods, participant observation—in other words—constitutes a *humanistic* methodology, a necessary adaptation of science to the distinctive subject matter of human studies (see Bruyn, 1966; Johnson, 1975; Douglas, 1976). Some recent advocates of ethnographic research see this debate over the scientific status of participant observation as a premodern phase of its history (see Denzin, forthcoming; Clifford and Marcus, 1986; Rabinow, 1977; Van Maanen, 1983).

It is not entirely clear, however, as to precisely what is involved with the humanistic methodology of participant observation. There are at least two reasons for this situation. One, practitioners of participant observation have resisted formulating definitive procedures and techniques. Its practice has been regarded as artful and inappropriate for any kind of linear, mechanical presentation. People interested in learning participant observation have been encouraged to become apprentices to a master practitioner, review classic studies exemplifying it, and go into the field and learn from direct experience (see Wax, 1971). For many of its zealous practitioners, participant observation is an art form and almost literally a way of life appropriately constituted as an oral tradition. Two, even when the methodology of participant observation has been discussed explicitly and presented in the form of textbooks, a fairly diverse set of characteristics have been emphasized. Dimensions such as the insiders' world of meaning, the natural environment of daily life, gaining entree, developing relationships, cultivating informants, participating, observing, and other forms of gathering information, logics of discovery and induction, and interpretative theorizing have received selective and differential treatment (see Hinkle and Hinkle, 1954; Lindeman, 1923; Palmer, 1928; Webb and Webb, 1932; Junker, 1960; McCall and Simmons, 1969; Lofland, 1971; Schatzman and Strauss, 1973; Spradley, 1980; Hammersley and Atkinson, 1983).

Developing a conception of participant observation for presentation here necessarily required making certain decisions and compromises. The methodology of participant observation is for me an abiding preoccupation—if not a way of life—and an important component of my social identity. You need not make such a commitment, however, to use participant observation appropriately and profitably.

All forms of scientific inquiry inevitably involve a wide variety of nonrational, extrascientific factors, and depend on artful judgments, decisions, and skills (see Watson, 1968; Cicourel, 1964, 1968, 1974; Garfinkel, 1967; Knorr-Cetina and Mulkay, 1983). This is especially true for participant observation because its practice fundamentally depends on the ability of the researcher to adjust and adapt skillfully to concrete conditions of daily life (see Johnson, 1975, 1977). Some people, partly because of their ability to interact and develop relationships with people quite easily, take more readily to participant observation than people without these abilities. For these same reasons, some people make better participant observers than other people.

The logic of participant observation is nonlinear, its practice requires the researcher to exercise a wide variety of skills, make judgments, and be creative, and many nonrational factors influence most aspects of actual study (see Johnson, 1975; Douglas, 1976; Reimer, 1977). Participant observation cannot be presented simply as a series of highly mechanical steps that, when followed literally by just anyone, will result without exception in competent participant observational research. None of this is to say, however, that participant observation cannot or should not be presented in a straightforward and entirely practical fashion. The conception of participant observation developed here explicitly treats nonrational influences on the researcher and research by alerting the practitioner to them and encouraging him or her to address these influences openly and honestly, especially when presenting findings. Likewise, the artful character of participant observation is readily acknowledged, and practitioners are encouraged to cultivate appropriate interpersonal skills as well as related abilities to think and act with sensitivity and creative judgment in the field.

It has not been possible to reconcile positivist and humanist conceptions of science. The editors of this series would have preferred that I present a more catholic or generic conception of participant observation. I have toned down polemics between participant observation and positivist methods, stressing the distinctive character of participant observation without developing certain comparisons and contrasts. There is nothing to prevent the reader from using participant observation simply as a method of collecting data within an otherwise positivistic conception of theory and research. Such a use of participant observation fails to utilize the full power of this methodology, but otherwise nothing bad happens if you do this.

It has not been possible to present participant observation, however, as anything but a thoroughly humanistic methodology while remaining true to myself and longstanding traditions of its practice. *Direct involvement in the here and now of people's daily lives provides both a point of reference for the logic and process of participant observational inquiry and a strategy for gaining access to phenomena that commonly are obscured from the standpoint of a nonparticipant.* This point and related dimensions of participant observation depend heavily on existing literature and traditions, especially as developed in American anthropology and sociology (see Hinkle and Hinkle, 1954; Wax, 1971;

Emerson, 1983). The conception of participant observation presented here is intended, however, to provide a coherent, unified perspective on this methodology, not merely an eclectic collection of borrowed elements. I agree with Denzin (forthcoming) that participant observation currently is undergoing radical transformation as its practitioners seek to integrate ideas of the postmodern era. I strongly disagree that this requires a complete rejection of existing traditions, or that there no longer will be a need for methods and methodology.

A conception of participant observation is presented in Chapter 1. Chapter 2 discusses and illustrates the unique logic of participant observational inquiry. Subsequent chapters discuss specific aspects of the methodology of participant observation: gaining entrée to human settings (Chapter 3); participating (Chapter 4); developing and sustaining field relations (Chapter 5); observing and gathering information (Chapter 6); making and maintaining notes, records, and files (Chapter 7); analyzing findings (Chapter 8); and leaving the field and communicating findings (Chapter 9).

Many people deserve mention in connection with this work. Margrette L. Nelson encouraged my early involvement in sociology and use of participant observation. These interests were further nourished, invigorated, and given a critical dimension by Gisela J. Hinkle. The idea of this book originally was suggested by Stephen P. Turner, who provided encouragement throughout the project. John M. Johnson and David L. Altheide directly influenced my thinking about and practice of participant observation. They introduced me to Jack D. Douglas and his writings, many of which are extremely important for current understandings of this methodology. They also constitute the center of an important circle of contemporary field-workers, with whom I have been privileged to participate. Joseph A. Kotarba, Peter Adler, and Carolyn S. Ellis read and provided valuable comments on the manuscript. Carol Rambo's experiences with becoming the phenomenon required me to rethink this strategy. I am hopelessly indebted to the very talented person responsible for typing, editing, and otherwise getting this manuscript in readable form. I happily and gratefully acknowledge the debt, even while I honor her request not to be named here. I gratefully acknowledge the invaluable assistance of Sam Fustukjian, Director of the Nelson Poynter Memorial Library of the University of South Florida at St. Petersburg, and the staff—especially Helen Albertson, Jackie Shewmaker, and Tina Neville—in locating and obtaining relevant literature. Julie, Greta, Adrean, Eric, and Mikkey keep me constantly in touch with the realities of daily life. Lin's spirited companionship ensures that my life ultimately is meaningful.

This work is dedicated to the memory of Bruce Edward (November 7, 1955-March 15, 1980), who was unable to make meaningful his continued existence.

—Danny L. Jorgensen

1

The Methodology of
Participant Observation

This chapter introduces and defines the methodology of participant observation. Uses and limitations of participant observation are identified and described. The methodology of participant observation is defined and illustrated by seven distinguishing features. Throughout this chapter, participant observation is compared and contrasted with other methodologies and methods, particularly experiments and surveys.

USES OF PARTICIPANT OBSERVATION

The methodology of participant observation is appropriate for studies of almost every aspect of human existence. Through participant observation, it is possible to describe what goes on, who or what is involved, when and where things happen, how they occur, and why—at least from the standpoint of participants—things happen as they do in particular situations. The methodology of participant observation is exceptional for studying processes, relationships among people and events, the organization of people and events, continuities over time, and patterns, as well as the immediate sociocultural contexts in which human existence unfolds.

Participant observation is especially appropriate for scholarly problems when

—little is known about the phenomenon (a newly formed group or movement, emotion work, fundamentalist Christian schools, improvised human conduct);
—there are important differences between the views of insiders as opposed to outsiders (ethnic groups, labor unions, management, subcultures such as occultists, poker players, or nude beachers, and even occupations like physicians, ministers, newscasters, or scientists);
—the phenomenon is somehow obscured from the view of outsiders (private, intimate interactions and groups, such as physical and mental illness, teenage sexuality, family life, or religious ritual); or

— the phenomenon is hidden from public view (crime and deviance, secretive groups and organizations, such as drug users and dealers, cultic and sectarian religions).

The methodology of participant observation is not appropriate, however, for every scholarly problem. Questions about fairly large populations, the precise causal relationships among limited sets of variables, and measurable amounts of something are better addressed by other methods, such as surveys or experiments. Participant observation is most appropriate when certain minimal conditions are present:

— the research problem is concerned with human meanings and interactions viewed from the insiders' perspective;
— the phenomenon of investigation is observable within an everyday life situation or setting;
— the researcher is able to gain access to an appropriate setting;
— the phenomenon is sufficiently limited in size and location to be studied as a case;
— study questions are appropriate for case study; and
— the research problem can be addressed by qualitative data gathered by direct observation and other means pertinent to the field setting.

Participant observation is especially appropriate for exploratory studies, descriptive studies, and studies aimed at generating theoretical interpretations. Though less useful for testing theories, findings of participant observational research certainly are appropriate for critically examining theories and other claims to knowledge.

FEATURES OF PARTICIPANT OBSERVATION

The methodology of participant observation consists of principles, strategies, procedures, methods, and techniques of research. Participant observation is defined here in terms of seven basic features:

(1) a special interest in human meaning and interaction as viewed from the perspective of people who are insiders or members of particular situations and settings;
(2) location in the here and now of everyday life situations and settings as the foundation of inquiry and method;
(3) a form of theory and theorizing stressing interpretation and understanding of human existence;

(4) a logic and process of inquiry that is open-ended, flexible, opportunistic, and requires constant redefinition of what is problematic, based on facts gathered in concrete settings of human existence;

(5) an in-depth, qualitative, case study approach and design;

(6) the performance of a participant role or roles that involves establishing and maintaining relationships with natives in the field; and

(7) the use of direct observation along with other methods of gathering information.

Ultimately, the methodology of participant observation aims to generate practical and theoretical truths about human life grounded in the realities of daily existence.

THE INSIDERS' VIEWPOINT

In the course of daily life, people make sense of the world around them; they give it meaning and they interact on the basis of these meanings (Schutz, 1967; Blumer, 1969; Denzin, 1978). If people define a situation as real, it is real in its consequences (Thomas and Thomas, 1928). People, of course, may be "mistaken" about what something means, yet even erroneous beliefs have real consequences. The world of everyday life constitutes *reality* for its inhabitants, natives, insiders, or members (Lyman and Scott, 1970, 1975; Berger and Luckmann, 1966). The insiders' conception of reality is not directly accessible to aliens, outsiders, or nonmembers, all of whom necessarily experience it initially as a stranger (Schutz, 1967; Simmel, 1950).

It is not possible to acquire more than a very crude notion of the insiders' world, for instance, until you comprehend the culture and language that is used to communicate its meanings (Hall, 1959, 1966). Greater comprehension requires that you understand the words of a language as they are used in particular situations (see Hall, 1976). Insiders manage, manipulate, and negotiate meanings in particular situations, intentionally and unintentionally obscuring, hiding, or concealing these meanings further from the viewpoint of outsiders (Goffman, 1959, 1974; Douglas, 1976).

The methodology of participant observation focuses on the meanings of human existence as seen from the standpoint of insiders (Znaniecki, 1934; Spradley, 1980). The world of everyday life as viewed from the standpoint of insiders is the fundamental reality to be described by participant observation. Put still differently, the methodology of participant observation seeks to uncover, make accessible, and reveal the meanings (realities) people use to make sense out of their daily lives. In placing the meaning of everyday life first, the methodology of participant observation differs from approaches that begin with concepts defined by way of existing theories and hypotheses.

Ellis (1986) became a participant observer in two Chesapeake communities for the purpose of describing everyday life activities within these fishing communities from the perspective of its members. Latour and Woolgar (1979) and Lynch (1985) described the insiders' conception of laboratory science using participant observational methods. Through participant observation, Mitchell (1983) described the experiences and meanings of mountaineering from the insiders' viewpoint. Kleinman (1984) used a participant observational methodology to reveal the meanings of seminary life from the standpoint of insiders. Chenitz and Swanson (1986) advocated participant observation for developing theories grounded in practice that are useful for nursing. Gallimeier (1987, forthcoming) focused on meanings and experiences of professional hockey players on the basis of participant observation of this sport. In short, then, the methodology of participant observation provides direct experiential and observational access to the insiders' world of meaning.

THE WORLD OF EVERYDAY LIFE

The world of everyday life is for the methodology of participant observation the ordinary, usual, typical, routine, or natural environment of human existence. This world stands in contrast to environments created and manipulated by researchers, as illustrated by experiments and surveys. In comparison with their natural habitat, animals are known to behave and interact differently in environments (such as a zoo or a laboratory) constructed and manipulated by researchers. Human beings likewise behave differently when they know they are being studied, especially when the researcher is very obtrusively manipulating the environment (see Roethlisberger and Dickson, 1939; Douglas, 1976; Douglas et al., 1980).

The *here* and *now* of everyday life is important to the methodology of participant observation in at least two fundamental ways. One, that is where the researcher begins with the process of defining and refining issues and problems for study. Two, they are where the researcher participates. No matter the original source of the study problem (abstract theory, practical experience, coincidence, or whatever), precisely what will be studied and how it will be regarded as problematic must be clarified and refined by reference to human existence in everyday life situations. Similarly, the researcher participates and observes in everyday life situations. Every effort must be made to minimize the extent to which the researcher disrupts and otherwise intrudes as an alien, or nonparticipant, in the situations studied. Taking the role of a participant provides the researcher with a means of conducting fairly *unobtrusive* observations.

Sanders (1988), for instance, participated directly in four tattoo parlors as a "regular" while observing this everyday life environment. To study the social world of preschool children, Mandell (1988) participated with and observed children on playgrounds, in classrooms, hallways, bathrooms, and lunchrooms of two day-care centers. Hockey (1986) studied the culture of enlisted men in the British Army from the concrete situations and settings of initial recruitment and basic training, to daily life in an infantry battalion, patrol in Northern Ireland, and rambunctious off-duty social life. To study stress and mental health as well as design an appropriate intervention strategy in a southern Black community, Dressler (1987) participated in and observed this environment, gathered information from key informants, and recruited research assistants and consultants from the community being studied.

INTERPRETATIVE THEORY AND THEORIZING

The methodology of participant observation aims to provide practical and theoretical truths about human existence. From this standpoint, a "theory" may be defined as a set of concepts and generalizations. Theories provide a perspective, a way of seeing, or an interpretation aimed at understanding some phenomenon (see Blumer, 1969; Agar, 1986). The methodology of participant observation provokes concepts and generalizations formulated as interpretative theories. These concepts and generalizations may be used to examine critically existing hypotheses and theories. Concepts, generalizations, and interpretations inspired through participant observation are useful for making practical decisions (see Chenitz and Swanson, 1986; Williams, 1986).

Interpretative theory differs from conceptions of theory aimed at explanation, prediction, and control of human phenomena (see Douglas et al., 1980; Polkinghorne, 1983; Agar, 1986). Explanatory theories are composed of logically interrelated propositions. Ideally, they contain lawlike propositions providing causal explanations. Explanatory approaches to theorizing stress the testing of propositions (or hypotheses) anticipating relations among concepts (see Wallace, 1971; Gibbs, 1972; Blalock, 1971).

Explanatory theorizing, especially in the form of hypothesis testing, involves a "logic of verification" (Kaplan, 1964). This logic operates by (1) the definition of a problem for study in the form of a hypothesis or hypotheses derived from or otherwise related to an abstract body of theoretical knowledge, (2) the definition of concepts contained in these hypotheses by procedures for measuring them (called operationalization), and (3) the precise measurement of concepts, preferably *quantitatively* (by degrees or amounts). Experiments and many forms of survey research, for instance, are employed for the purpose of testing hypotheses and explanatory theories.

Altheide (1976), to illustrate, conducted a study of television news through participant observation. He was interested in bias or distortions in news making. Having reviewed relevant scholarly literature, Altheide was aware of several different perspectives on this issue, as well as specific contentions (hypotheses) explaining why or how news is biased. He suspected that bias was somehow related to how news workers put together television news programs. With this general idea, but without specific hypotheses (operational definitions or measures), Altheide set out to describe news workers' images of their jobs and how they actually did their work. His findings describe in qualitative detail how practical and organizational features of doing news work promote ways of looking at events that distort them. The emergent, interpretative theory of the news perspective as bias provided a solid, empirical basis for questioning the accuracy of some previous claims (if not the complete rejection of these hypotheses) and reinterpreting other theoretical claims. This study, furthermore, resulted in subsequent research and refinement of Altheide's interpretative theory of news making (see Altheide, 1985; Altheide and Snow, 1979).

The participant observational study of delinquents by Emerson (1969) resulted in the more general concept of "last resorts" (Emerson, 1981). Suttles's (1968) participant observational study of slums led to theorizing about communities (Suttles, 1972). Irwin's (1970) participant observational study of prisoners resulted in a typology of felons and a theoretical critique of contemporary prisons. Fox's (1987) participant observational study of "punks" resulted in a typology of punk status and a general conception of the informal stratification of this antiestablishment subculture. Goffman's (1961) highly influential theoretical concept of "total institutions" emerged from participant observation in a hospital (see also Richard, 1986).

AN OPEN-ENDED LOGIC AND
PROCESS OF INQUIRY

Participant observational inquiry may proceed on the basis of some more or less abstract idea or it may derive from involvement with a field setting. Either way, what is problematic must be defined or redefined specifically by reference to the actual study setting. The methodology of participant observation stresses a "logic of discovery," a process aimed at instigating concepts, generalizations, and theories (Kaplan, 1964). It, in other words, aims to build theories grounded in concrete human realities (Glazer and Strauss, 1967; Agar, 1986). This requires a flexible, open-ended process for identifying and defining a problem or problems for study, concepts, and appropriate procedures for collecting and evaluating evidence.

The methodology of participant observation encourages the researcher to begin with the immediate experience of human life in concrete situations and settings, and make the most of whatever opportunities are presented (see Whyte, 1984). Scott (1968), for instance, took advantage of a longstanding interest in horse racing to conduct a participant observational study of the racing game. While the researcher may have a theoretical interest in being there, exactly what concepts are important, how they are or are not related, and what, therefore, is problematic should remain open and subject to refinement and definition based on what the researcher is able to uncover and observe. This process and logic of inquiry requires the researcher to define the problem of study and be constantly open to its redefinition based on information collected in the field. It further encourages the researcher to define concepts by providing elaborate *qualitative* descriptions of them in terms of what people do and say in everyday life situations.

Wallis (1977), for instance, used participant observation to gather information on Scientology concerning a set of "broad themes" rather than hypotheses. Weppner (1983) participated in an addiction treatment program prior to defining problems precisely for further study. Much like Weppner, Sudnow (1978) studied and played jazz piano before making the organization of improvised conduct the subject of study. In other words, Sudnow's special interest in how improvised conduct is organized and accomplished partly derived from and was informed by his piano-playing experiences.

IN-DEPTH CASE STUDIES

Case studies take a variety of forms, most of which do not involve participant observations (see Yin, 1984). The methodology of participant observation, however, generally is practiced as a form of *case study*. This involves the detailed description and analysis of an individual case (Becker, 1968, pp. 232-38). Case studies stress the holistic examination of a phenomenon, and they seek to avoid the separation of components from the larger context to which these matters may be related. The case studied may be a culture, society, community, subculture, organization, group, or phenomenon such as beliefs, practices, or interactions, as well as almost any other aspect of human existence. Gans (1962), for instance, studied the case of urban villagers. Lofland (1966) studied the case of religious conversion. Becker et al. (1961) studied the case of student medical school culture.

Case studies conducted by way of participant observation attempt to describe comprehensively and exhaustively a phenomenon in terms of a research problem. Scholarly definition of the problem generally provides a logic justifying study of a single case. The phenomenon, for instance, may be sufficiently important or unique to justify intensive investigation. Whether or not, or to the extent to which, the case is representative of some larger population may be regarded as not especially relevant, or this matter simply may be left open to further study. Comparative case studies generally depend on previous studies of a single case. Ellis (1986), for instance, participated in two fishing communities. This enabled her to compare and contrast different cases. The logic of the case study clearly differs from the survey research emphasis on gathering data on a large cross section of some population, or the emphasis of experiments on demonstrating causation by control and comparison of variables.

For some participant observational studies, questions concerning representativeness or possible bias resulting from study of a single instance receive further attention (see Douglas, 1985). The researcher may have good reasons for focusing on a single case, such as an argument that it is "typical," among other bases for sampling theoretically (Glazer and Strauss, 1967). The use of nonprobability (or theoretical) sampling techniques also applies to selective observations conducted *within* a case. Although participant observational case studies generally do not employ conventional methods of probability sampling, such techniques certainly may be used. Participant observation in this way differs from most forms of survey research, as well as from experiments that use probability to select subjects.

Hochschild (1983), for instance, was interested in the private and public face of human emotions, or simply "emotion work." This study was exploratory and aimed to generate theory. Partly for this reason, Hochschild conducted an in-depth case study—based on a participant observational methodology—of emotion work, rather than conducting an experiment or some form of survey research.

Theoretical logics were used to select phenomena for study. Initially, a questionnaire was used like a fishing net to catch indications of ways people manage emotions. Hochschild had a variety of good theoretical reasons for participating as a flight attendant while observing: emotion work is especially important in service occupations; flight attendants are neither high nor low prestige; and male flight attendants make possible gender comparisons. Interviews were conducted with people in this industry (union officials, pilots, bill collectors, a sex therapist, a receptionist, recruiters, managers, and other attendants) partly to gain different existential perspectives on emotion work. Even the selection of Delta Airlines was justified theoretically; its standards were higher and its worker demands lower than other companies. Emotion work was more visible and sharper in this exaggerated instance. Hochschild does supplement the Delta data, however, with observations of several other airlines, thereby checking for too extraordinary results.

THE PARTICIPANT ROLE

The methodology of participant observation requires that the researcher become directly involved as a participant in peoples' daily lives. The participant role provides access to the world of everyday life from the standpoint of a member or insider. Human meaning and interaction is approached through sympathetic introspection (Cooley,

[1930] 1969), verstehen (Weber, 1949), a humanistic coefficient (Znaniecki, 1934), or sympathetic reconstruction (MacIver, 1942). Participant observation, in other words, is a very special strategy and method for gaining access to the interior, seemingly subjective aspects of human existence (see Krieger, 1985). Through participation, the researcher is able to observe and experience the meanings and interactions of people from the role of an insider.

Participant involvements may range from the performance of nominal and marginal roles to the performance of native, insider, or membership roles (Junker, 1960; Gold, 1954, 1958, 1969). The researcher's involvement may be *overt* (with the knowledge of insiders), *covert* (without the knowledge of insiders), or—most likely—insiders selectively will be provided with knowledge of the researcher's interests and purposes (see Adler and Adler, 1987; Adler, Adler, and Rochford, 1986). It is highly desirable for the participant observer to perform multiple roles during the course of a project, and gain at least a comfortable degree of rapport, even intimacy, with the people, situations, and settings of research.

As a participant, the researcher must sustain access once it has been granted, and maintain relationships with people in the field (see Johnson, 1975). The relationship between the participant as observer, people in the field setting, and the larger context of human interaction is one of the key components of this methodology. The character of field relations heavily influences the researcher's ability to collect accurate, truthful information.

Hayano (1982), for instance, became a professional cardplayer (became the phenomenon studied) as part of his participant observational investigation of poker players. Similarly, Sudnow (1978) became a jazz pianist to study improvised conduct. Hayano and Sudnow, it should be noted, were interested in poker playing and jazz piano for important biographical (or personal) reasons not directly related to scholarly concerns. Forrest (1986) used apprenticeship strategically as a participant observer role. Peshkin (1986), on the other hand, nominally participated in activities at a fundamentalist Christian school studied while observing and retaining the identity of a researcher. Likewise, Wallis's (1977) participation in Scientology was limited to a brief training period. Douglas became a nude beacher to study this scene, but he also participated as a member of the home owners' association opposed to the nude beach (Douglas and Rasmussen, with Flanagan, 1977). Hayano, Sudnow, and Wallis participated covertly for the most part, while Peshkin's participant role was entirely overt. Douglas did not reveal his research interests (and certainly not his participation as a nude beacher) to the home owners, but, depending on the circumstances, his everyday life identities sometimes were acknowledged to the nude beachers.

METHODS OF COLLECTING INFORMATION

Direct observation is the primary method of gathering information, but the participant observer usually uses other strategies. Depending on the nature and extent of participant involvement, the researcher's immediate experience can be an extremely valuable source of data (Cooley, [1930] 1969; Znaniecki, 1934, pp. 157-67). Documents (newspapers, letters, diaries, memoranda), as well as other forms of communication (audio recordings, photography, videotapes, radio, television) and artifacts (art, tools, clothing, buildings) are readily available in many field settings. The researcher may find informants knowledgeable about matters of interest, and gather life histories (Thomas and Znaniecki, 1918-19). Participant observers commonly gather data through casual conversations, in-depth, informal, and unstructured interviews, as well as formally structured interviews and questionnaires (see Fine, 1987; Wallis, 1977).

Participant observation may be conducted by a single researcher. Or researchers may employ a team strategy (see Lynd and Lynd, 1929; Warner and Lunt, 1941, 1942; Warner and Srole, 1945; Warner, 1959; Vidich and Bensman, 1968; Becker et al., 1961). Team strategies offer distinctive advantages, such as the possibility of performing different participant and observer roles simultaneously as well as exploiting various talents and identities (such as gender) of the researchers (see Golde, 1970; Douglas, 1976; Douglas and Rasmussen, with Flanagan, 1977; Warren and Rasmussen, 1977).

It is extremely important that the results of participant observational study be recorded. Participant observers generally keep a diary or log of activities in the field, unique experiences, and other matters of possible interest. The researcher may keep written records or tape-record observations while in the field or shortly after some period of observation. Action may be recorded by way of photographic, audio, and/or audio-video equipment. Increasingly, computers have been employed to record, file, and otherwise assist in the organization and analysis of research materials (see Conrad and Reinhartz, 1984).

Hochschild (1983), to illustrate, used questionnaires, several forms of interviewing, and direct observation in studying emotion work. Wallis (1977) depended extensively on documents, used a questionnaire, conducted informal interviews, and briefly participated as an observer in collecting data on Scientology. Fine (1987) participated and observed among Little Leaguers, and used a questionnaire. Altheide (1976) used direct observation and formal and informal interviewing, collected documents and newscasts, and engaged in natural experiments in studying news making. Hayano (1982), in studying poker players, depended primarily on observation and memory, making records after a period of intense participation. Johnson (1975) recorded the results of direct observation and informal interviews on an audio recording during and after periods of participant observation of welfare workers. Spradley (1970) used direct observation, informal and formal interviews, a life history, and depended on native informants for information on urban alcoholics.

SUMMARY

The methodology of participant observation is appropriate for a wide range of scholarly problems pertinent to human existence. It focuses on human interaction and meaning viewed from the insiders' viewpoint in everyday life situations and settings. It aims to generate practical and theoretical truths formulated as interpretative theories. The methodology of participant observation involves a flexible, open-ended, opportunistic process and logic of inquiry through which what is studied constantly is subject to redefinition based on field experience and observation. Participant observation generally is practiced as a form of case study that concentrates on in-depth description and analysis of some phenomenon or set of phenomena. Participation is a strategy for gaining access to otherwise inaccessible dimensions of human life and experience. Direct observation and experience are primary forms and methods of data collection, but the researcher also may conduct interviews, collect documents, and use other methods of gathering information.

Participant observation is appropriate for a wide range of problems, especially when the meanings people use to define and interact with their ordinary environment are central issues. Though especially useful for exploratory and descriptive research purposes, participant observation results in generalizations useful for forming new theories as well as testing existing ones. The methodology of participant observation differs considerably from positivistic approaches, especially experiments and surveys.

Unlike participant observation, experiments demand control and manipulation of the research environment. Experiments are best suited for testing specific hypotheses and theories conceived in terms of causal relationships among quantitatively measured variables. Unlike participant observation, experiments are highly obtrusive and not especially useful for exploratory purposes. Survey research is best suited for collecting a vast amount of information regarding public opinion as well as basic (demographic) characteristics of populations (see Babbie, 1973; Fowler, 1984).

Survey questionnaires or interviews enable the researcher to collect a standardized set of data, much of it in quantitative form, from relatively small samples of subjects. Probability sampling techniques enable the researcher to generalize these findings to larger populations. Like experiments, survey research is useful for testing theories and providing explanations.

EXERCISES

For the purpose of these and subsequent exercises in this book, you will need to become familiar with literature illustrating participant observational research. You will find the list of references at the end of the book useful in locating books and articles. Journals publishing the results of participant observation include *Administrative Science Quarterly, American Anthropologist, American Behavioral Scientist, American Journal of Sociology, Current Anthropology, Human Organization, Journal of Contemporary Ethnography* (formerly *Urban Life*), *Qualitative Sociology, Social Problems, Sociological Quarterly*, and *Symbolic Interaction.*

1. Select several illustrations of participant observational research, either monographs or journal articles. Examine and discuss these illustrations in terms of interpretative theorizing, a focus on human meaning and everyday life activities, in-depth case study design, the participant role, and the use of observation and other strategies for collecting information. To what extent do they illustrate these basic features of participant observation? To what extent do they differ with one another?

2. Select a journal article or book illustrating (a) a participant observational study, (b) an experiment, and (c) survey research. Identify and discuss similarities and differences among these methodologies. How are they alike or different, specifically, in terms of issues such as problem formation, conceptualization, measurement, sampling, strategies and procedures of data collection, analysis, and theorizing?

3. Select one or more illustrations of participant observational research and discuss the ways that this methodology was or was not *appropriate* for the problem, questions, or issues studied. Would it be possible to investigate these issues by way of some other strategy? If so, what might have been the principal differences between these approaches?

4. Identify a research problem. Suppose, for instance, that you are interested in the relationship between children's home environments and school adjustment and performance; or perhaps a problem like drug usage among factory workers; or the effectiveness of an alternative school for pregnant teenagers; or a social problem like gambling; or—better yet—supply your own problem. Discuss how participant observation might be used to study this research problem. What are the advantages and disadvantages of participant observation for the investigation of the problem?

2

The Process of Defining a Problem

This chapter discusses and illustrates the logic and process of defining a problem. Procedures for formulating concepts and specifying indicators are outlined and exemplified. Validity and reliability are discussed in terms of the methodology of participant observation. The process of problem definition is located within the human context of values, politics, and ethics of research.

THE SOCIOCULTURAL CONTEXT OF RESEARCH

Kuhn's (1970) classic work on the history of science leads to an appreciation for sociocultural and historical influences on scientific work (see, also, Knorr-Cetina and Mulkay, 1983). Because of its special subject matter, the importance of this relationship is compounded for the human sciences. Participant observation, in arguing that human studies require a unique methodology (one placing the researcher in direct contact with people in everyday life settings), involves a reconsideration of values, politics, and ethics as important influences on research. A decision to engage in participant observation requires some consideration of these issues.

Values and Politics

All science aims to arrive at true and objective findings. Bias, prejudice, and personal (or subjective) opinions pose a threat to truth (and objectivity). Scientific methods are thought to be ways of guarding against the influence of values and politics. Because the human sciences, unlike the physical sciences, deal with subjective, value-laden phenomena, the need for value-freedom has been seen as especially important. While human science never completely achieves this ideal, it conventionally is held to be a worthy goal.

The methodology of participant observation shares the goal of accurate and truthful findings. It disagrees, however, that truth can be achieved in any absolute sense, or by merely conforming to proper procedure, and it rejects the possibility of value-freedom even as an ideal (Johnson, 1975; Douglas, 1976; Adler and Adler, 1987). Scientific work always involves values, and it commonly is political. Truth, therefore, is a constant problem. Explicit discussions of the actual procedures and processes scientists use to achieve "truth," while providing no absolute guarantees, are necessary.

What values participant observation (or science) should be committed to can only be settled by discussion among scholars, and then never absolutely. Furthermore, while in principle we may agree to certain values—such as freedom or justice—exactly how these principles apply in particular cases oftentimes will be problematic, requiring further discussion. In doing participant observation, the researcher needs to consider what values—those of the researcher as well as other participants—are involved, and what implications these values hold for truthful findings. These questions, furthermore, must be addressed constantly, during all phases of research from the conceptualization of a problem to the final report of findings.

There is no necessary conflict between personal, subjective interests or values and the scientific goal of truth (see Psathas, 1973; Rabinow, 1977; Hunt, 1984; Krieger, 1985). Personal interests hold potential for new insights and creativity inspired by emotional and intellectual identification with the topic of study (Johnson, 1975, 1977). These interests may be what sustains a participant observer through months or even years of demanding labor. Rather than denying personal interests and values, the methodology of participant observation requires an awareness of how these thoughts and feelings influence research. By reporting personal interests and values, other people are able to evaluate further the influence of values on your findings.

Ferraro's (1981) interest in wife battering arose from her personal experiences with battering. Her participant observational study of battered women and the shelter movement combined biography, efforts to intervene in this social problem, and sociological research. There is no indication that the objectivity of her study suffered because of this combination of interests. Just the contrary, Ferraro's battering experiences enabled her to establish rapport quickly and very satisfactorily with battered women.

The methodology of participant observation rejects the conventional conception of and distinction between subjectivity and objectivity. Gaining access to the *subjective* reality of everyday life—the world as it is experienced and defined by insiders—is required for accurate and truthful findings. Objectivity, defined as truth, cannot be achieved without coming to terms with the insiders' world. The most direct route to truth is for the researcher to experience the phenomenon of interest— to "become the phenomenon" (see Mehan and Wood, 1975; Douglas and Johnson, 1977; Adler and Adler, 1987). Less direct, but highly appropriate strategies include direct observation and means, such as interviewing, for gathering information from the people whose daily lies are of interest.

Ethics

There has been much discussion of the ethics of research involving human beings, some of it directly concerned with participant observation (see, especially, Adler, Adler, and Rochford, 1986; Klockars and O'Connor, 1979; Bulmer, 1982; Cassell and Wax, 1980). Research ethics center on the value of human life and rights of the individual. Scientists agree that people should not be physically harmed by research, and codes of ethics in different fields have been designed on this basis. Aside from physical harm to subjects, ethical codes generally prohibit violations of people's right to privacy, confidentiality, and freedom from exploitation.

While there is little disagreement with these principles, participant observers have debated their application in particular situations. They have argued that, unlike experimental psychology or medicine, partici- pant observation does *not* have human subjects. In other words, the people with whom the participant observer interacts are not at all like the subjects of an experiment or even the respondents of survey research. The participant observer interacts with people under the ordinary conditions of their daily lives much like any other participant. The participant observer's interest in research, though different, is not unlike any number of special interests people have in interacting with one another. Consequently, the participant observer has no more or less of an ethical obligation to the people encountered in the course of research than she or he would have under other everyday life circum- stances. While this does not free the reseacher from responsibility for his or her actions as they might affect other human beings, the researcher is not necessarily obligated to inform people of research intentions, or even protect them from possible harmful consequences. Taylor (1987), for instance, faced the dilemma of what to do when observing abuse of mentally retarded patients. Reporting abuse might harm the abusers, lead to an end of research, and possibly have little beneficial effect on the patients.

Studies of crime and deviance would be extremely difficult, if not impossible, if participant observers were required to announce their research purposes constantly. What people and interests will be protected? Are people (like drug addicts or prostitutes) to be protected from themselves? Is the participant observer required to protect criminals who sell illegal goods or commit violent crimes? Should people be protected from their own beliefs in, for instance, fundamentalist religion or the occult?

These decisions and choices are easy to make only in contexts removed from everyday life, such as textbooks. Participant observers are deeply concerned with ethics, but they see ethical norms as guidelines that require application in particular situations. As with truth, there is no way of absolutely ensuring ethical research. Like values and politics, research ethics are matters of constant concern as the participant observer identifies a problem for study, gains access to everyday life situations, participates, interacts, and develops relationships with other human beings.

GETTING STARTED

A unique advantage of participant observation is the use of observation and experience in the field to clarify and define precisely what is going to be taken as the problem for inquiry. While having a general idea about the topic and issues of possible interest, the participant observer depends on information collected in the field to define and focus the problem to be studied. Exactly what will be studied is defined by reference to what insiders do and say in everyday life. Participant observation requires the researcher to *learn* about the insider's way of life as it is experienced, defined, and made meaningful by him or her. Though important, a review of literature is only a small part of the process of defining a problem for participant observation. As the problem changes and is refined, it generally is necessary to refer repeatedly to relevant literature.

From Problem to Setting

Participant observation may proceed on the basis of a problem identified prior to research in a field setting. You may have a more or less general idea about what is to be studied, the issues involved, and the ways that it is problematic before going into the field. This problem may be derived from personal interest, scholarly concerns (perhaps related to some abstract body of knowledge or theory), a topic uncovered during other research, or a matter viewed as problematic by other people (such as government officials, policymakers, reformers, or administrators). When going into the field with an idea about what is problematic, it is important to remain open to the widest possible range of findings, including the possibility that your initial idea is inappropriate or completely mistaken.

Participant observation is especially useful for studies aimed at applying knowledge. Hughes (1977), for example, faced the difficult challenge of developing a program for heroin addicts. He reasoned that knowing more about the daily existence of addicts might result in information useful for designing an effective treatment program. A research team was formed and, using participant observation, they investigated this general issue and developed specific questions. Knowledge about the daily lives of street addicts gathered through participant observation indeed was useful in developing effective strategies for intervention with addicts in a community setting (see Hughes, 1977).

In many forms of applied research, such as evaluation studies, the researcher is given some general problem or set of issues and asked to develop a more specific plan of study, including the formulation of specific questions or hypotheses. Hebert (1986), for instance, was responsible for evaluating two innovative educational programs concerned with language and cultures. The general research problems were known: one study called for an evaluation of the impact and consequences of a program; while the other study involved a needs assessment. Hebert employed participant observation to *negotiate* specific study questions and issues as well as to collect appropriate evaluation data. This study underscores the value of participant observation in providing appropriate strategies for defining and refining study questions and problems, negotiating these issues with different constituent groups, and collecting information. Hebert also used participant observation successfully as a basis for dealing with the politics of these programs and different interest groups as well as providing general education about the issues involved. Similarly, Woods (1985) argues that participant observation may be used to train teachers. Getting them to think like observers as well as participants facilitates a reflective process helpful for understanding teaching.

In proceeding from a problem to more specific issues and questions defined by field participation, the researcher may realize that the initial question is somehow inappropriate (it just does not make sense in terms of the realities of everyday life), or that many important issues in need of study were not anticipated at the outset. For example, I (1979) set out to study "extraordinary claims to knowledge." Guided by general theoretical perspectives (interactionism, ethnomethodology), I planned to find some marginal religious group and study the interactional procedures used by people to achieve the sense that they had accomplished extraordinary knowledge, as with spirit communication, prophecy, divination, and so on. During the search for an appropriate setting, I found it necessary, partly for practical reasons, to learn more about where practitioners were located and how their activities were (or were not) organized. Although completely unplanned, I ended up conducting a thorough study of these issues (see Jorgensen, 1979, 1982, 1983; Jorgensen and Jorgensen, 1982) before returning to the original question (see Jorgensen, 1984).

From Setting to Problem

Participant observation does not necessarily proceed from the definition of a problem to location of an appropriate setting for study. People quite commonly develop scholarly interests and problems for study through ordinary participant involvements in daily life. Similarly, participant observers select field settings at least partly because of previous involvement. Adler (1981), for instance, became an assistant college basketball coach and later decided to conduct participant observation as part of a study of momentum in sport. Rambo (1987) was an exotic dancer—an occupation in which she engaged to pay for an undergraduate education—and later she used this experience as the basis for formal study, including subsequent participant observation. Hayano (1982) was a poker player before defining professional card playing as a research problem. Kotarba (1977, 1980, 1983) suffered from back problems for many years. He tried acupuncture and later used this experience to write a research paper. His everyday life experiences eventually led to an extensive participant observational study of chronic pain and health practitioners.

Starting with a setting requires the researcher to define and analyze emergent findings for specific matters of interest and further study. To illustrate, Adler (1985) was a sociology graduate student with an interest in deviance, but she was not out looking for instances of drug dealing to study. Partly as a matter of chance, she noticed the activities of a neighbor and correctly interpreted these cues (based on previous personal and scholarly experience) as drug dealing. She told a professor about this dealer and was encouraged to cultivate this emergent social relationship for scholarly advantage.

Adler (and her spouse) became friendly with the drug dealer, leading to her introduction to his friends, many of whom also were involved in the dealing scene. Adler's growing involvement with people connected to this scene led to greater and greater participation, and through direct personal involvement to her initial formulation of questions of possible interest. These questions were not formed as hypotheses, but rather they emerged through participant interaction with the setting and discussions of what she was observing with her spouse, professors, and other scholars. Explicit formulation of research questions and issues took the form of notes and records based on field observation and discussion. She began questioning, for instance, who was involved in this scene, the extent of their involvement in drug dealing, the manner in which the scene was organized, and so on.

In seeking answers to these questions, Adler generated an even larger set of related questions and issues for study. This process eventually results in a greatly expanded set of research interests and, commonly, more questions than can be answered by the research. Decisions consequently have to be made about what issues to pursue, what issues to set aside for the time being, what issues to leave out entirely, and the awareness—through lack of certain knowledge—that you probably are missing many other possible issues for study. There are few absolute rules to making these decisions. Ultimately, they may be arbitrary, even though the participant observer should have good theoretical reasons for focusing on one set of issues over and against any number of other possibilities. In other words, you should be able to defend to a professional audience the questions and issues selected for study.

AN ONGOING DEFINING PROCESS

What is taken to be the problem for research by participant observation is the result of a flexible, open-ended, ongoing research process of identifying, clarifying, negotiating, refining, and elaborating precisely what will be studied. Early research efforts should be concentrated on gaining access to appropriate situations for observation, gathering information, and even analyzing results. Leaving study questions open-ended is not an excuse for sloppy problem definition. You should have a basic idea about what phenomena to study, as well as a vague notion, at least, about possible results. Leaving the problem open-ended creates further difficulties and responsibilities, not present when a problem is stated as a hypothesis.

Your problem statement should be sufficiently broad to permit inclusion of the central issues and concerns, yet narrow enough in scope to serve as a guide to data collection. You must exercise caution that the problem is sufficiently focused and defined so as to be manageably investigated, given finite money, time, and other resources, as well as the characteristics of the problem itself, such as accessibility of an appropriate setting. Preliminary problem statements may be formulated very usefully as a question to be addressed.

There is a real danger that, as you become immersed in the setting and overwhelmed by what transpires there, you will find it increasingly difficult to stand back and generate a fruitful perspective on what is of interest. Should this happen, you will spend an incredible amount of process of identifying, clarifying, negotiating, refining, and elaborating precisely what will be studied. Early research efforts should be concentrated on gaining access to appropriate situations for observation, gathering information, and even analyzing results. Leaving study questions open-ended is not an excuse for sloppy problem definition. You should have a basic idea about what phenomena to study, as well as a vague notion, at least, about possible results. Leaving the problem open-ended creates further difficulties and responsibilities, not present when a problem is stated as a hypothesis.

Your problem statement should be sufficiently broad to permit inclusion of the central issues and concerns, yet narrow enough in scope to serve as a guide to data collection. You must exercise caution that the problem is sufficiently focused and defined so as to be manageably investigated, given finite money, time, and other resources, as well as the characteristics of the problem itself, such as accessibility of an appropriate setting. Preliminary problem statements may be formulated very usefully as a question to be addressed.

There is a real danger that, as you become immersed in the setting and overwhelmed by what transpires there, you will find it increasingly difficult to stand back and generate a fruitful perspective on what is of interest. Should this happen, you will spend an incredible amount of valuable observational energy without a sense of purpose or direction. Eventually this leads to frustration, lack of interest, confusion, and in some cases the premature end of what might have been an important study.

After a reasonably short period of observation, your questions should be reevaluated. Did they lead to relevant observational materials? Were they relevant to the insiders' perspective? Have additional questions emerged from observation? If you are unable to provide substantive and positive answers to these questions, more than likely the problem will need to be reformulated. If, on the other hand, the initial questions produce positive results—even, or especially, if these results were unanticipated—the research is moving in a fruitful direction, and a variety of possible leads probably will be uncovered.

Appropriately formulated questions result in such a wealth of data that you will realize it is impossible to study all matters of potential interest. During early stages of research, it may be possible to change entirely the direction and focus of the project in response to unanticipated findings without an unreasonable loss of time and effort. It is very likely, moreover, that this basic process will be repeated innumerable times as research continues. Indeed, while the defining process sometimes results in a discernible end point (the central objectives have been accomplished to a large extent), more often than not there is no clearly marked end point. Rather, you come to realize that research might continue indefinitely. Should this happen, you will have to make a relatively arbitrary decision about drawing closure on the field observation portion of the project. This decision is greatly facilitated by having questions that you have or have not addressed adequately. In short, then, defining a problem for participant observation is a complex process through which you refine and elaborate the issues to be studied while participating and collecting information in the field.

FORMULATING CONCEPTS AND
SPECIFYING INDICATORS

As what you are studying becomes more focused, it is appropriate to formulate key concepts for further study and specify how these concepts are indicated. The data of participant observation generally take the form of fairly detailed, *qualitative* definitions and descriptions. Basic concepts are defined *phenomenologically*: that is, in terms of what these ideas and actions mean to people in particular situations. Indicators of key concepts likewise involve a search within the field context for meaning, relevancy, and linkages of key concepts and ideas (see Bruyn, 1966). In formulating concepts based on the insider's perspective, participant observers seek out multiple indications (or indicators) of what an idea means, including how it is used (see Glazer and Strauss, 1967).

Participant observers rarely define concepts operationally, measure concepts quantitatively, or analyze these materials statistically. Operational definitions preconceive what will be found and thereby obscure insiders' meanings, resulting in profound misunderstandings (Agar, 1986). Quantification risks distorting everyday life realities (unless meanings are viewed by insiders in quantitative terms). Insofar as operational definitions and quantitative measures are appropriate for participant observation, they tend to be used only after the researcher has gained considerable familiarity with the insiders' world, or as a supplementary research strategy.

A central objective of participant observational research is the definition of key concepts in terms of the insiders' perspective. Anthropologists have developed formal strategies for discerning the meaning of folk concepts, in part at least, of the linguistic expressions whereby experiences of everyday life are mediated symbolically and communicated in a meaningful fashion to other people. A first step to describing a culture, subculture, or way of life is to make an *inventory* of the key words used by members of this culture. Next, specific words are analyzed by asking members to describe how the word is used or simply observing how symbnols are used. This generally entails further observation or questioning pertinent to what is included in this linguistic domain, as well as noting what things are similar to and different from the symbol or word in question.

Spradley (1970), to illustrate, was interested in the social world (or subculture) of urban nomads. Outsiders refer to these people in terms of labels such as derelict, wino, and transient. To health care practitioners, they are alcoholics. From a legal standpoint, they are drunks or vagrants. And for social scientists, they are homeless men. The men themselves, however, use the word "tramp" and they make extremely important distinctions about themselves. A "tramp," for example, may be a bindle stiff, airdale, rubber tramp, home guard tramp, box car tramp, or ding. Still other kinds of tramps are mission stiffs, of which there are nose divers and professional nose divers, and working stiffs, including construction tramps, sea tramps, tramp miners, and fruit tramps.

By starting with the labels employed by these people to identify and describe themselves, Spradley focused specific attention on this way of life from the perspective of insiders. Relevant concepts emerged from field observation. Aside from notions of social identity, Spradley observed daily activities, particularly contacts with the legal system. He focused on the processes whereby urban nomads come into contact with police and end up in jail, a process insiders call "making the bucket." This way of life involves complex meanings associated with serving a jail sentence or "doing time." Spradley proceeded by asking a series of informal and preliminary questions about the way of life of urban nomads. Through participant observation, these questions received further definition and refinement, leading to more specific subsequent questions. He thereby was able to identify particular concepts and processes as part of this way of life. Further observation then was focused on uncovering the meaning of these concepts from the insiders' point of view, and discerning their relationship to the daily life and culture of tramps.

Validity and Reliability

Concept formulation raises the important matters of validity and reliability (see Becker, 1969; Glazer and Strauss, 1967; Wiseman, 1970; Douglas, 1976; Kirk and Miller, 1986). It is extremely important when defining concepts nominally (by single dimensions or the most obvious characteristics) to examine and test the extent to which the concept actually reflects everyday life meanings and usage. This issue is rarely problematic for participant observation because of the preoccupation with defining concepts by what they mean and how they are used by people in everyday life. Participant observation, in other words, results in highly *valid* concepts.

Questions regarding concept validity in participant observation revolve around whether or not the researcher has been able to gain direct access to the insiders' world of meaning and action (see Adler and Adler, 1987). Participant observation, furthermore, requires the researcher to collect multiple indicators (or forms of evidence) regarding key concepts. It is very important to describe conflicts and disagreements over the meanings of basic concepts, and otherwise note differences among insiders. Actual use of the concept in the field during interaction with natives provides a very powerful test of the validity of concepts. Successful use of the concept strongly suggests that you have described it accurately, while objections to your usage by natives suggest inaccuracy (Altheide, 1976).

The reliability of participant observation sometimes is questioned. Defined conventionally, reliability refers to the extent to which a procedure, especially measurement, produces the same result with repeated usage. A lack of consistent results raises serious questions about the scientific value of any procedure or method. Approaches, like participant observation, that stress concept validity generally anticipate a corresponding decrease in reliability. Consistency of results is more likely to be obtained when the procedure is simple, routine, and highly standardized, as with most forms of quantitative measurement, even though this frequently results in certain sacrifices in concept validity, especially if the concept is very complex and otherwise difficult to measure accurately by standard instruments.

In principle, procedures used in participant observation can be expected to result consistently in the same findings. Yet these methods tend to be uniquely adapted to particular settings and questions. In practice, consequently, it is exceptionally difficult to establish reliability by the conventional process of repeated usage of the technique (as the standard test of reliability of procedures like measurement). Given that participant observation rarely involves measurement, conventional notions of reliability are not especially appropriate.

The methodology of participant observation is very much concerned, however, with *dependable* and *trustworthy* findings. Viewed in this way, reliability is very much interrelated with validity. The validity and reliability of participant observation may be checked in a number of ways (see Wiseman, 1970).

— The participant observer, as already noted, rarely depends on a single form of evidence. Concepts are formulated and checked by multiple procedures and forms of evidence, such as direct experience and observation, different forms of interviews, and different informants, artifacts, and documents.

— It is extremely important to ask whether or not and the extent to which the researcher's procedures have provided direct access to the insiders' world. Limited access generally results in less valid and reliable findings.

— The methodology of participant observation, more than most scientific approaches, requires the researcher to describe and discuss fully the procedures used to collect information. The researcher thereby is obligated to discuss for the reader the relationship between the procedures employed and the results obtained, including advantages and limitations of these procedures.

— Explicit, detailed discussion of study procedures subjects them further to *public* examination and scrutiny. In other words, study procedures are subject to debate and testing in the experience and judgment of everyone reading the final report.

— Important concepts may be tested by actual usage in everyday life, as noted above. It is difficult to imagine a more severe test of the accuracy or dependability of an idea than that it pass the test of use in everyday life.

— Although it may be difficult in practice, in principle there is no reason why the methods of participant observation cannot be checked by independent restudy.

Validity and reliability, in short, then, are closely interrelated issues that acquire a distinctive character for the methodology of participant observation. Unlike approaches stressing nominal definitions and measurement, participant observation emphasizes real definitions and multiple indicators of key concepts. Dependable and trustworthy results are a fundamental concern, and participant observation provides a number of strategies for checking for valid and reliable findings.

SUMMARY

The methodology of participant observation is characterized by a flexible, open-ended strategy of defining a problem for study by reference to people's daily lives. You may begin with a general problem and define it further through participant observation in an appropriate setting. Or you may begin with a human setting and generate problems for study through participant observation. In either case, study problems are stated in the form of questions to be addressed, refined, elaborated, and focused further through data collection. Concepts are derived from the meanings people use to make sense of their daily existence. In other words, concepts are defined phenomenologically. Emergent concepts are indicated by what people do and say in concrete situations. Participant observation results in highly valid concepts. Because participant observation generally does not involve measurement, reliability—as conventionally defined—is not an issue. Participant observation, however, is concerned with reliability—conceived of as dependable and trustworthy findings.

The methodology of participant observation recognizes that science transpires in the value-laden and highly political context of human association. Like all science, it aims for accurate and truthful findings. Unlike other approaches, it rejects the idea that scientists can or should be free from values or refrain from becoming involved subjectively and personally with the phenomena studied. By constantly seeking an awareness of their personal and professional interests in human life and making explicit the actual procedures used to produce factual information, participant observers confront the issue of truthful results directly and publicly. Participant observation, likewise, seeks constantly to become aware of the rights of the people whose lives are studied and the consequences of research for these people and their way of life. Research ethics, in other words, is a daily concern of the participant observer.

EXERCISES

1. Briefly identify and state a problem for possible participant observational study. Indicate the origins of this problem, or how you arrived at this problem. In what ways is this problem influenced by (a) personal or biographical factors, (b) existing theories or research, (c) social problems, or (d) other possible factors? Discuss the ways that your interests limit or facilitate participant observation. In what ways would this research raise ethical considerations? How would you deal with ethical issues?

2. Select a piece of research illustrating a participant observational approach to problem definition and another exemplifying the testing of a hypothesis or hypotheses. Compare and contrast these approaches to problem formulation, conceptualization, and measurement. Why and how are these approaches appropriate for the problems studied?

3. Identify some topic to be clarified, elaborated, and defined further by participant observation. Discuss some of the ways you might go about specifying and defining this topic more exactly as a problem of inquiry. What kinds of difficulties would you expect to encounter in doing this? How would you deal with these troubles?

4. Select several examples of participant observational research from the literature. In what ways do these studies raise the issues of validity and reliability? How were these issues dealt with? Discuss why and how the treatment of validity and reliability were or were not appropriate.

3

Gaining Entrée to a Setting

This chapter discusses and illustrates gaining entrée to a human setting for participant observation. Features of everyday life settings, including politics, are described. Strategies for selecting and gaining entrée to appropriate settings are discussed and exemplified. Procedures for observing more or less selectively or comprehensively within a setting are outlined and discussed.

SELECTING A SETTING

Selection of a setting is interrelated with the problem studied. The interconnection between problem and setting is balanced deliberately and systematically, through the process of defining and elaborating the study problem by reference to the setting. Although the study problem is subject to change, the researcher participates unobtrusively in everyday life. Because the setting does not change, it is very important to consider carefully the implications of selecting a particular setting for study.

In proceeding from a general problem to selecting an appropriate setting, the ways a proposed setting will limit and facilitate the issues you anticipate investigating should be evaluated. Common sense generally provides a sound basis for these decisions. It is perhaps obvious that there is a limited range of settings appropriate for researcher problems concerned with, for instance, Christian schooling, drug addiction, or teenage pregnancy. The more you know about a setting, the easier it is to make an informed decision about whether or not it will be possible to investigate the topic of interest. Partly for this reason, participant observers commonly explore a variety of possible settings at least casually while anticipating whether or not the setting is appropriate for the research problem. I observed and participated in occultism in several different cities before deciding on a study setting. Peshkin (1986) observed several fundamentalist Christian schools and was denied research access before locating the setting he studied.

The decision to participate in a setting, as previously noted, sometimes is based on opportunity and convenience. Indeed, the researcher already may be a participant before deciding formally to conduct research in the setting. Molstad (1986), for instance, worked for extended periods of time in the beer bottling industry prior to making boring work the topic of scholarly inquiry. In arriving at this decision, you still need to consider the ways in which the setting limits and facilitates what may be investigated. This judgment, of course, takes you directly into the process of defining a problem for study. You may decide, however, that in spite of convenience and opportunity the setting is not sufficiently interesting or appropriate for research.

The selection of a setting for participant observation, furthermore, is contingent on (1) whether or not you can obtain access to the setting, (2) the range of possible participant roles you might assume, and (3) whether or not this role (or roles) will provide sufficient access to phenomena of interest. Here again, the more you know about possible settings, the easier it will be to make informed choices. The decisions ultimately require action by the researcher in concrete situations. You cannot know, for instance, whether or not you will be permitted to observe a setting until you try it.

It is also important to consider your own interests and abilities. Will you be able to participate and observe effectively within this setting for sufficient time to gather the desired information? You may find the setting boring or personally offensive. You may be unwilling or unable to perform the available participant roles. Gaining access to the setting, participating, or establishing and sustaining relations with insiders may tax your abilities and resources beyond reasonable limits.

For instance, in seeking a setting for my (1979) study of occult claims to knowledge, I planned to find a particular group—everyone knows that sociologists study groups. I found participation with most groups to be unpleasant. As a scientist, these beliefs and practices, though very entertaining, were difficult to take seriously, especially during sustained periods of intimate interaction with members of a group. I began to question whether or not it would be possible to conduct the study as planned. Fortunately, I resolved this difficulty by performing a series of roles (seeker, client, occult practitioner) that placed me in direct contact with the occult milieu—eventually as a fully participating insider—and did not require ongoing involvement with a particular cultic group. Though entirely unplanned at the outset, this adaptation to the conditions of field study actually facilitated detailed study of a larger set of phenomena (networks of occultists) than would have been possible had I found and remained involved with one group.

FEATURES OF SETTINGS

Access to a field setting depends on features of these human arenas. A field setting may be *visible* or *invisible* from the standpoint of the general public, and it may be more or less *open* or more or less *closed* to outsiders. These characteristics of human settings also apply to particular situations within a setting. Some occasions, in other words, will be open to almost anyone, while other occasions will be closed to just anyone. Similarly, some situations within a setting will be readily visible to almost everyone, while other situations will be largely invisible to all but a few people. These characteristics of field settings, as implied here, vary by degree, and they occur in various combinations.

Visible to Invisible

The visibility of particular aspects of human life depends on where you are located, as well as on your previous knowledge and experience. A setting is visible when information about it is available to a general public. Wright (1978), for instance, found it easy to participate in and observe planned demonstrations but more difficult to be present at unplanned outbursts of collective behavior, like riots, even though these phenomena were entirely public. Visible settings, such as universities, hospitals, mental health clinics, and churches, usually are listed in the telephone book. Some settings are visible but less observable. Unruh (1983) notes that lives of the aged commonly are invisible. Drug dealers and addicts, prostitutes, delinquent gangs, bikers, gay people, swingers, and occultists may be visible if you know where to look (see Ponse, 1976; Warren, 1974).

While information about these settings usually is not listed in the telephone directory as such, in most American cities it is more or less public. Drugs, prostitutes, and gay bars may be located by talking with police, cab drivers, or hotel employees (See Delph, 1978; Milner and Milner, 1972). Information about delinquent gangs is available from police and school employees. Police and motorcycle businesses frequently have information about biker clubs. Swingers and occultists may be located through book and supply stores specializing in sexually explicit materials or the occult.

Some human settings are almost entirely invisible from the standpoint of outsiders. These settings are hidden, concealed, and obscured from the view of outsiders. This knowledge even may be a secret protected by insiders (see Bellman, 1984). Activities of bikers, delinquent gangs, drug dealers, as well as groups of swingers and occultists, for instance, may be carefully concealed from the view of all but the most trusted members. Secret activities and groups also exist, of course, in more respectable society. Within almost every complex organization, for instance, there are cliques of people whose activities are kept secret from nonmembers. Locating these settings is extremely difficult without prior experience with more visible aspects of these human scenes. This knowledge may be acquired by gaining the trust and confidence of an insider willing to talk with you.

Open to Closed

A human setting is more or less *open* if access to it requires little negotiation. A setting is more or less *closed* if access requires considerable negotiation. Some settings are almost entirely closed to an overt research approach, leaving the participant observer with a decision either to forgo investigation or to find some way to negotiate access covertly. Whether or not a setting is open or closed to participant observation is only partly related to its visibility. Simply because a setting is highly visible, as in the case of hospitals, universities, corporations, and many other complex organizations, certainly does not mean that it is open to public inspection. Likewise, because a setting is only partly visible to outsiders does not mean that it is closed to participant observation.

Human activities in settings such as public parks, beaches, streets, and areas for spectator sports tend to be readily visible and open to any observer with sufficient knowledge of American culture to know where to look. Highly visible public settings, however, frequently contain less visible activities. Public parks and beaches may conceal activities such as sexual interactions that otherwise are closed. Similarly, the otherwise open and public character of street life may hide illegal activities, such as drug deals, sexual contacts, and gambling.

Goffman (1959), likening collective existence to a drama, distinguishes between "frontstage" as opposed to "backstage" regions of human settings. While some settings, such as public dining rooms, are almost entirely front stage, other settings, such as nonpublic bathrooms or the bedroom of a home, largely are backstage regions. Most human settings, however, are neither entirely visible and open (frontstage), nor entirely invisible and closed (backstage). Most human settings instead contain both front-stage and backstage regions.

Entrée to visible, frontstage settings generally is open to anyone willing to become a participant. Spectator sports are observable for the price of admission. Almost anyone may observe a criminal trial— presuming you know where and when to find it. Access to these settings may be gained by assuming the role of spectator, a role readily available to most people. Each of these settings, however, also contains backstage regions closed to just anyone. Access to a sport's locker room, for instance, requires special permission. Not everyone is invited into the trial judge's chambers. Although many aspects of a large corporation may be open to almost anyone, certainly not all of the activities going on therein are open to the participant observer as an outsider.

Politics

Most human settings are to some extent political (see Douglas, 1976; Punch, 1986). In other words, they involve the use of power by people. In human settings, furthermore, people are ranked by values associated with the positions they occupy and the roles they perform. Human settings generally are stratified: Differential amounts of prestige are attached to people based on their status and role (see Wax, 1979). Power and prestige usually are related: People with more prestige tend to have greater power than people accorded less prestige. Power and prestige within human settings commonly are the source of conflict and disagreement, sometimes among rival factions (see Vidich and Bensman, 1968).

The politics of gender and its influence on fieldwork has received much needed attention in recent years (see Golde, 1970; Easterday et al., 1977; Warren and Rasmussen, 1977; Pastner, 1982). Being female enhances fieldwork in many situations, particularly by providing a perspective different from that of men in societies dominated by a male outlook (see Wax, 1979). In some situations, however, being a female participant observer may present serious obstacles, such as in studies of predominantly male occupations, subcultures, or cultures (see Hunt, 1984; Horowitz, 1983). Being a male researcher generally presents fewer obstacles for participation, depending on the setting and situation. Male participant observers, however, need to be more fully conscious that their gender roles limit (as well as facilitate) what may be observed in particular settings and situations (see Warren and Rasmussen, 1977).

Failure to notice and respond appropriately to these aspects of human settings may create serious difficulties for the participant observer (see Whyte, 1984). It usually is not possible to sustain friendly relations with rival parties under conditions of extreme conflict (see Bromley and Shupe, 1979; Kornblum, 1974; Jacobs, 1977; Dalton, 1959, 1964). Similarly, it usually is not possible to sustain cooperative relations with people of disparate rank. During any extended time period, access to the activities of one faction or strata of a setting most likely will prohibit similar access to the activities of rival factions or unequal strata.

For instance, overt access to an organization usually requires seeking permission from people in authority (of high prestige). Although subordinates may be required by their superiors to permit you to observe, it is difficult to prevent them from resenting your presence, or engaging in tactics designed to obscure your view. In a factory setting, the workers may assume that you are a management spy sent to observe their activities. Consequently, you may have to decide between forgoing observation and covertly gaining entrée to the organization as a worker.

In short, then, human life tends to be political and stratified. These features of human life may influence gaining access to settings of interest as well as other aspects of the research. The participant observer should be alert to the possible consequences of politics and stratification within human settings and should be prepared to adjust strategies of entrée and participation on this basis.

ENTRÉE STRATEGIES

There are two basic strategies for gaining access to human settings. When the researcher openly requests permission to observe, the strategy is called *overt*. This direct approach to entrée is preferred because it raises few ethical problems, is less difficult than other approaches, and, when granted, tends to provide adequate access to phenomena of interest (see Whyte, 1984; Hilbert, 1980). It sometimes is not possible to negotiate overt entrée, and sometimes this strategy fails to provide appropriate access to phenomena of interest. The other basic strategy for gaining entrée—especially to settings closed to outsiders—is *covert*. In this case, the researcher assumes some participant role without informing people in the setting that research is under way (see Douglas, 1976).

The decision to employ an overt or a covert strategy for gaining entrée is a delicate one. If the researcher employs a direct approach and is denied access, it may not then be possible to enter the setting covertly. This decision, therefore, requires that the researcher have some knowledge of the politics of the setting and an ability to judge tentatively the likelihood of success using a direct approach. Covert observation is ethically controversial, and it contains the very real possibility that participant observation in the setting will be terminated if the investigative interest is discovered (see Bulmer, 1982). Many researchers also find it difficult to manage interaction with people under conditions wherein their research intentions must be concealed.

Overt Strategies

There are many ways of gaining overt entrée to human settings depending on the setting and the resourcefulness of the researcher. The most ideal situation is one in which authorities and other people in the setting welcome the researcher (see Warner and Lunt, 1941, 1942; Warner and Srole, 1945). Under most circumstances, overt access is gained by seeking permission from the highest possible authority, and gradually convincing them, as well as other people in the setting, that the researcher can be trusted.

In seeking permission to participate and observe, the researcher should present the appropriate authority (board, director, and so on) with a copy of a proposal to do participant observational research. This proposal should outline the basic plan of the research, the basic goals and purposes, provide good reasons why it is in the interest of the authority to permit the research, and treat any issue likely to be used as grounds for denying the request, such as matters of a politically or ethically sensitive nature, or any apprehensions about the dissemination of findings.

Because possible grounds for denial may be difficult to foresee, it is extremely useful to discuss these issues informally with authorities prior to presenting the formal proposal. A most useful strategy for gaining access is to gain the trust and confidence of an authority in the setting. Good initial relationships with such people can be invaluable as they may be willing and able to become powerful advocates from within the setting for the would-be participant observer. Perhaps needless to say, the more that people in the setting, especially those in positions of authority, are prepared to support the research, the more likely is access to the setting.

Depending on the setting and the researcher, it may be possible to use the prestige of the researcher (as an authority, a scientist, and so on) and the prestige of the subject matter or discipline. An appeal to the authority of the researcher or the discipline obviously is more likely to be successful when these matters are valued by people in the setting. It is helpful to have the support of people whose opinions are valued by the authority, or people whose opinions the authority must respect for perhaps purely political reasons—such as when the supporting party has some legislative or economic control over the setting.

If permission initially is denied, it may be possible for the researcher to uncover the grounds for this decision. Minor changes in the proposal may be all that is required to gain permission, although you may be faced with more serious compromises to the original plan. Once permission has been granted to conduct participant observation, it certainly may be withdrawn later. As will be discussed in the next several chapters, entrée is only a step in a much larger process requiring the researcher to maintain friendly relationships with people in the field. Unless access to the setting and cooperation of the people therein can be maintained, participant observation obviously is unlikely to be successful.

For instance, Warner's (1959) access to Yankee City was facilitated by community leaders. Key informants helped Whyte (1955) to gain access to street-corner activities and helped Anderson (1978) to gain entry to Jelly's Bar. Similarly, Liebow's (1967) access to the insiders' world of Tally's corner was facilitated by a key informant who served as a sponsor.

Covert Strategies

To some participant observers, covert tactics absolutely are unethical and thereby unacceptable under any circumstances (see Bulmer, 1982). In this view, covert participant observation involves deceiving insiders because they are not informed of the research. Aside from being dishonest, covert strategies violate the norm of informed consent because people are unable to agree to participate in the research. Covert strategies thereby fail to respect the rights of human subjects. These objections notwithstanding, most participant observers agree that covert strategies at least are necessary under some circumstances, such as in studies of deviant or criminal subcultures. Other participant observers have defended the use of covert strategies as essential to acquiring truthful information. In this view, human existence itself is full of conflict, dishonesty, and self-deceptions. If participant observers, they argue, always were required to announce their research interests, studies of most areas of human life would be impossible or at best restricted to the public fronts employed by people to manage impressions of human life and existence (Douglas, 1976).

Participant observation, unlike survey research or experiments, as was noted in the last chapter does *not* have human "subjects." Rather, situations in which human beings are involved are observed under otherwise natural conditions. Furthermore, while people may be the source of information, they are not manipulated or controlled in any way resembling the design of other kinds of research. Participant observers have been careful to respect the dignity and anonymity of people observed in the field, oftentimes performing services or paying people in exchange for information. And there are many instances of researchers becoming involved in some human situation or setting as a matter of personal interest, and only later deciding to conduct participant observational research formally. Unless potential researchers were required to warn everyone they encountered that they might end up doing research, under such conditions it would be impossible to avoid at least some unintentional deception.

Not everyone is informed of the research interest (and true purpose of research) even when an overt strategy is employed. Conversely, even when a setting is approached covertly, it is likely that at least a few people eventually will be provided with information pertinent to the research aims. Hence, a covert strategy may be employed largely for the purpose of gaining unobtrusive access to some setting. Once the researcher has established trusting relationships, people may be told of the research interests (see Fine, 1987).

Although researchers tend to worry about gaining access to hidden or secretive phenomena, such as marginal religious groups, deviance, or criminality, it generally is more difficult to gain access to the backstage regions of otherwise public and frontstage settings. Religious groups, secret societies, deviance, and crime generally are accessible to people who know where to look and who are willing to become participants.

Access in these cases, of course, may depend on the researcher's willingness to participate and observe covertly. Religious groups, secret societies, and subcultures of deviants are open to outsiders under particular conditions, but this is not to say that these people will grant permission to be studied.

Access to the backstage regions of otherwise visible and public phenomena, such as factories or corporations, may be possible by taking a position in the setting and observing covertly. Depending on the problem and the setting, however, even this option may not be available. If the research problem, for instance, concerns the deliberations of corporate boards, only board members are present at these deliberations, and if the researcher is not a board member, then even covert strategies for gaining entrée are unlikely to be successful. Covert access to a setting is constrained by whatever roles are available and assumable by the researcher. The researcher, in other words, is required to find and assume some position readily available within the setting. This may be as simple as assuming the position of a potential recruit or newcomer, or as complex as having to learn a specialized role for the purpose of disguised access and observation.

For instance, to study teachers' classroom images, Clandinin (1985) participated as a classroom aide. Broadhead (1983) took advantage of living among students in professional programs to gain access to their private, personal lives. A House of Representative's fellowship enabled Freudenburg (1986) to conduct participant observation of congressional culture.

Gaining access to a setting is one of the most difficult and demanding aspects of participant observation, yet it provides much room for creative engagement by the researcher. Successful entry to a setting depends on his or her interpersonal skills, creativity, and commonsense decision making. It has been possible to outline some basic dos and don'ts of entry, as well as call attention to some likely problems, political issues, and ethical considerations, but there is no substitute for creative judgments by the researcher in the field. Ultimately, every field setting and situation is at least slightly different and unique. Masayuki Hamabata (1986), for instance, manipulated his identity to gain access to Japanese culture. A third-generation Japanese American, Masayuki Hamabata learned to speak Japanese. In Japan, he first presented himself as an American. Once accepted as an outsider, he switched to a more Japanese identity, resulting in partial acceptance as an insider.

COMPREHENSIVE AND SELECTIVE OBSERVATION

Selecting a setting for study and identifying situations to be observed within a setting are decisions about what phenomena will be observable. It is never possible to observe every possible setting or even every situation that is of interest within a setting. Convenience, opportunity, and the interests as well as the abilities of the researcher influence these decisions. These decisions, furthermore, should be defensible theoretically.

Theoretical or *judgmental* sampling is a form of nonprobability sampling that depends on the researcher's ability to make decisions about what to observe based on constraints such as opportunity, personal interest, resources, and, most important, the problem to be investigated. As in probability sampling, the researcher develops a logic for selecting particular phenomena for study. What logic is appropriate depends on the nature of the problem to be studied. Different problems call for different reasons as to what phenomena are selected for observation. As in probability sampling, the researcher generally is able to estimate the likelihood that these observations are appropriate and representative of the phenomenon studied. Unlike probability sampling, the researcher is unable to sample or estimate error by recourse to a simple statistical formula.

The logic or strategy for sampling theoretically, as has been suggested, necessarily depends on the problem of study and the settings appropriate for observation. When what is problematic is defined and elaborated while the researcher explores a setting (or settings), the participant observer also is required to develop a strategy for observing through this process. Because participant observation commonly begins with an available instance of the phenomenon of interest, a frequently used logic is to generate additional cases for observation from a known instance or instances.

"Snowball" sampling, as this strategy is called, is especially useful when the phenomenon of interest is obscured, hidden, or concealed from the viewpoint of an outsider. The basic idea of snowball sampling is to obtain sufficient information from a known instance of the phenomenon to be able to identify and locate subsequent instances for observation. As the name suggests, phenomena for observation tend to grow like a snowball through this procedure. Many studies of crime and deviance have used a snowball procedure to generate a set of phenomena for study. Miller (1986), for instance, used a snowball sampling technique in a participant observational study of street women (including hustlers, prostitutes, and petty criminals).

Selecting phenomena for study on theoretical grounds is illustrated nicely by Sudnow's (1967) participant observational study of the social meanings of death. He wanted to know, specifically: How are decisions made about when, where, and how a death has occurred? There are a limited range of settings—hospitals, scenes of accidents, nursing homes, and so on—where this phenomenon might be observed. Sudnow consequently had good theoretical reasons for selecting a hospital.

There are different kinds of hospitals, however, and different locations in a hospital where death may be observed. Sudnow, partly as a matter of opportunity, initially observed a public hospital but later added a private hospital setting. Observation within the second setting enabled Sudnow to examine differences between these types of settings and check for possible bias in the public hospital data. Within a hospital, Sudnow's original observations were conducted in the emergency room, an obviously appropriate setting for observing social meanings of death. Because deaths also occur in other areas of a hospital, Sudnow also observed surgery and other locations of death.

Like Hochschild (1983), whose sampling strategy was discussed in the last chapter, Sudnow depended on opportunity, common sense, and theoretical logic in selecting a setting for observation and phenomena to observe within the setting. There is no reason to think that either Hochschild's or Sudnow's findings would be different if additional settings or situations for observation were added. Had Sudnow only studied the public hospital, this in no way would have detracted from the description of how death was defined. Changes he observed in the definitional process between the public and private hospitals settings were differences in degree, not kind. The process of deciding and defining death was the same fundamentally in both settings. In short, then, participant observers depend on professional judgments to select cases and instances within a case for observation.

SUMMARY

This chapter described and illustrated principles and strategies for gaining entrée to human settings for the purpose of research. What is selected for observation depends on the problem to be studied, possible settings and situations of study, available resources (such as time and money), opportunity, and personal interest. Human settings and situations within settings vary by the extent to which they are publicly discernible and accessible to outsiders. Settings and situations range on these dimensions from visible to invisible, front stage to backstage, and open to closed. The politics of most human settings and situations also must be considered in gaining access. Entrée may be approached overtly, by seeking permission to participate and observe, or covertly, by assuming a participant role and observing without asking permission. While many settings may be entered overtly, access to other settings is not possible except by a covert strategy. Participant observation commonly involves different degrees of overt and covert entrée and participation. Exactly what the participant role involves is the subject of the next chapter.

EXERCISES

1. Select a topic/problem from the following list: teenage pregnancy, high school dropouts, job burnout, conflict in organizations, welfare services. Identify possible settings where you might study the topic/problem selected. Discuss how and why particular settings are or are not appropriate for study. What, if any, difficulties would you anticipate in gaining entrée to these settings? How might these troubles be resolved?
2. Suppose you will be studying a setting (such as some form of crime, deviance, secret or private conduct) closed to outsiders. How might you go about gaining entrée to this setting? What, if any, political or ethical difficulties would you anticipate?
3. You have been hired to study drug use among high school students (or make up your own problem). Discuss how you might gain entrée by an overt and a covert strategy, comparing and contrasting these approaches. Do you favor one approach over the other? Why or why not?
4. From among the examples provided in these exercises, select a setting for study (or provide one of your own). Discuss what would be involved in selecting phenomena for observation from within the setting. In other words, how would you go about selecting phenomena for observation? Specify and defend your logic.

4

Participating in Everyday Life

This chapter discusses principles and strategies for participating in everyday life settings. It develops the idea that where the researcher is located with respect to phenomena of interest limits and facilitates what may be observed. Different views and forms of participating in human settings are described and illustrated.

LOCATION AND PERSPECTIVE

Where the researcher is located with respect to a phenomenon of interest *determines* what may be observed. From great distances phenomena look much different than they do from just a short distance away. They look different when viewed from different angles, such as from the side, the back, the top, or the bottom. What you are able to observe is influenced greatly by whether the experience is based on sight, sound, taste, smell, or various combinations of your senses. The more information you have about something from multiple standpoints and sources, the less likely you are to misconstrue it.

All observation is influenced by a person's physical location. For human studies, the *social location* of the researcher also is critically important. People are defined socially by where they are located in relationships to and in association with other people. The social location of a Black, middle-class, Moslem, university professor, spouse of a prominent businessman, and mother of teenaged children differs radically from the social location of a single, White, Catholic, male, with a criminal record who currently is an unemployed factory worker. *Where* the researcher is located socially determines *what* is observable, the character of observations, and opportunities to observe. Actions that appear to be totally meaningless from the social location of an outsider may be highly significant from the standpoint of an insider.

Every physical and social location provides a certain *perspective* on phenomena of interest. There is no perfect or ideal location or perspective. The adequacy of a participant role perspective depends on the problem to be studied. Every perspective contains inherent, built-in limitations and even biases. There is no absolute guarantee against inaccurate findings due to limited sight or experience, but the participant observer can be sensitive to how a role limits and facilitates observation. The participant observer should seek different angles and perspectives, constantly searching for information and evidence for critically examining emergent findings.

Johnson, to illustrate, tells about the child admitted to a hospital under conditions thought by the staff to be an instance of abuse. All of the evidence—the child's physical condition, the absence of both parents, and other contextual clues—pointed to a definition of "child abuse" from the staff's experienced perspective. Shortly, however, the mother arrived at the hospital, and her story resulted in a much different view. According to the mother (a professional nurse), the child had become severely ill in response to antibiotic treatment for a routine illness. A lengthy ordeal followed: The attending physician had sought to discover reasons for the child's reaction and a treatment plan; the mother eventually decided that this treatment was inappropriate; and, over the physician's objections, she insisted that the child be transferred to a metropolitan hospital.

The mother's initial absence was not, as originally defined, a sign of neglect, but simply a fact of arranging for the care of her other children and traveling a great distance, once emergency air transportation had been arranged for the ill child. The child's father too, she indicated, would be at the hospital shortly. At the metropolitan hospital, the child's condition was diagnosed as a negative reaction to antibiotics and she began responding to treatment. Hearing the mother's story, the medical staff revised their perception of child abuse, eventually concluding that the symptoms probably were due to medical malpractice.

The point of this illustration is not that a "correct" interpretation emerged. Available evidence commonly makes it difficult to decide between conflicting perspectives definitively. With the evidence initially available to them and from previous experience, the hospital staff arrived at a reasonable conclusion from their social location. The mother's perspective was quite different, of course, based on a different location and also access to additional information not available to the medical staff. Although Johnson did not have direct evidence of the rural physician's perspective, the indirect evidence certainly suggests that he had an entirely different viewpoint. Other perspectives were possible: Because the child was less than a year old, there was little possible access to her thoughts and feelings; neither did Johnson provide any indication of what the child's siblings thought or felt about the matter; he did not indicate if perhaps there were at least slight differences of opinion among the medical staff, especially among the physicians; and, as a social scientist, Johnson made sense of the situation as an instance of the process whereby people go about defining frequently ambiguous life situations. In abstracting this situation out of context and providing it with a set of meanings pertinent to the influence of social location on an observer's perspective, I have provided still another view of these events.

In short, then, different social locations provide different perspectives on matters of scholarly interest. Unlike the above example, it commonly is difficult or impossible to decide clearly and unambiguously what, if any, particular viewpoint is "correct." Participant observation aims to gain direct access to as many perspectives as possible. In other words, participant observation aims to gather the best possible evidence, knowing that rarely is any set of evidence "perfect" or even exhaustive of the meanings people apply to the circumstances of their daily lives.

IMAGES OF PARTICIPATION

Participant role may be conceptualized on a continuum from a *complete outsider* to a *complete insider*. Between these extremes, the researcher is an outsider or an insider to a greater or lesser degree. The participant role being performed defines the researcher's social location with respect to the phenomenon of interest. You may be located more or less on the outside of the phenomenon of interest or more or less on the inside. What the researcher is able to see, hear, touch, taste, smell, or feel is determined by participant role involvement.

In contrast with this view, four participant roles sometimes are identified (see Junker, 1960; Gold, 1958, 1969): a complete observer, a participant-as-observer (more observer than participant), an observer-as-participant (more a participant than observer), or a complete participant. Participation and observation, consequently, are seen as competing, and even conflicting objectives. The more you participate, the less you are able to observe, and vice versa. This view of participant observation discourages complete participation because subjective involvement is thought to be a threat to objectivity (Gold, 1958, 1969).

Supposed competition and conflict between observation and participation have been greatly exaggerated (see Johnson, 1975; Douglas, 1976; Adler and Adler, 1987). In our everyday lives, we routinely perform multiple roles more or less simultaneously. There may be times and circumstances when it is difficult to concentrate full attention on participating while also observing. Skilled and self-conscious investigators, however, are able to participate, intensively and extensively, at the same time they are experiencing and observing the world around them. Hence, ordinary experience contradicts the idea that as your participant involvement increases, your ability to observe effectively and accurately is diminished.

Accurate (objective and truthful) findings are *more* rather than less likely as the researcher becomes involved directly, personally, and existentially with people in daily life. Objectivity suffers when the researcher, due to a narrowing vantage point, fails to apprehend the meanings people attach to their existence. The potential for misunderstanding and inaccurate observation increases when the researcher remains aloof and distanced physically and socially from the subject of study. Participation reduces the possibility of inaccurate observation, because the researcher gains through subjective involvement direct access to what people think, do, and feel from multiple perspectives. Hall (1976), for instance, cites many, many cases of profound misunderstanding resulting from viewing other cultures from the severely limited perspective of one's own cultural vantage point. To see why other cultures regard time differently, it is necessary to become familiar with their view of time, for instance.

OUTSIDER ROLES

Entry to a human setting generally provides direct physical access to matters otherwise obscured from the standpoint of people totally outside the setting. As an outsider present at the scene, the participant observer gains a more advantageous location, yet under most circumstances he or she still lacks familiarity with what goes on within the setting. Initial naiveté is quite limiting, but it may be used to strategic advantage at the outset of inquiry. As an outsider looking in, you can overview a scene, noting major and distinctive features, relationships, patterns, processes, and events. This is extremely important, because insiders do not view their world from this standpoint, and once you become even somewhat familiar with the setting, its initial newness and strangeness also will be lost. Dollard (1937), for instance, laments the loss of this initial strangeness with which he experienced race relations in a southern town.

Overt participation as a researcher (outsider) permitted at the scene is a common role. Given that "researcher" almost never is a natural role, this form of participation is obtrusive and necessarily imposed on the setting. It provides, however, access to phenomena of interest and considerable freedom to concentrate on research. Overt participation, furthermore, is readily assumed, requires little adjustment to the investigator's self-concept, and raises few ethical problems. Participating as an outsider is appropriate for many scholarly problems.

For example, Vesperi (1985), a youthful anthropologist, was interested in the "old old" who, living in poverty, are dependent upon social services. St. Petersburg, Florida, a city with a high proportion of older people, served as a convenient location for her study as she was employed at a university campus across Tampa Bay. Because of her age, it was not possible for Vesperi to become a complete insider. Partly to gain a better viewpoint, she did take up residence in St. Petersburg and gathered data by interviews and through informants, as someone sympathetic to the daily lives of older people. In participating with these people, Vesperi performed a variety of roles: ordinary citizen, potential friend, and anthropological researcher. Sometimes she participated overtly (as a researcher), while at other times her research role was covert. In observing and talking with people sitting on benches in a park, interacting with one another in public, or walking down the street, there is little need to mention one's research interest unless people ask about it (see, also, Cottle, 1977). Like many participant observers, Vesperi performed a variety of roles, mostly as an outsider and researcher, strategically studying daily life among older people.

Berger's (1981) study of rural communards in northern California further exemplifies participant observation as a researcher-outsider. Although he participated as an outsider, members of the commune were accepting of his presence and even depended on Berger's professional expertise. The values of these people encouraged great toleration of other people, including researchers. Berger consequently was able to establish remarkable rapport with insiders while participating overtly as a researcher.

Peshkin (1986) also participated as a researcher/outsider in a study of fundamentalist Christian schooling. Like Berger, Peshkin did not become an insider. He was, however, able to establish considerable rapport with school administrators. Because of the character of fundamentalist beliefs, the level of rapport established by Peshkin was remarkable. Although the role of an outsider-researcher provided Peshkin with access to the insiders' world of meaning and action (especially administrators'), it limited his ability to gain access to the subworlds of teachers and students. The students' perspective, however, was grasped successfully by two assistants who conducted extremely candid interviews with students.

The politics of participating as an outsider may present problems. People tend to respond to you based on their preconceptions of a "researcher." Peshkin (1986), for instance, clearly had difficulty—much of it political in character—in gaining access to the perspectives of teachers. Partly this situation results from the highly obtrusive presence of any outsider. People interact with you as an alien who under more normal circumstances would not be part of their environment. This may result in displays of suspicion, contempt, hostility, indifference, curiosity, friendliness, or even deference, depending on the setting and how your presence is (or is not) legitimated.

An accurate picture of daily life requires that the presence of an outsider-researcher be routinized. Time generally is an ally: The longer (or more frequently) you are in the setting, the more people are likely to come to perceive you as nonthreatening and otherwise take your existence for granted. Casual interactions when not forced also tend to put insiders more at ease, especially if you are able to engage them in casual conversation and provide routine assurances that you pose no threat to them.

FROM OUTSIDER TO INSIDER ROLES

Although participating as a researcher places the observer on the margins of human action, it rarely is possible to remain uninvolved with insiders. People have a tendency to involve you, even if only in a token effort to put you at ease or perhaps demonstrate the superiority of their perspective over yours. You will quite likely be asked to contribute expertise, whether or not you feel qualified to do so, or otherwise assist in some way. Involvements with people indicate that you are being accepted to some extent as part of the setting. Participant involvement, in turn, suggests that what you are able to observe increasingly is what people normally say and do even when an outside observer is not present.

Johnson and several colleagues, for example, began riding with police as observers of family disputes and violence. Very quickly they were defined by the police as experts on the treatment of these problems, a role sometimes accepted also by the couples and families. So defined, they were expected to render assistance by arbitrating family disagreements and violence, citing principles of law, counseling family members, and making referrals to appropriate community agencies. This indicates that the researchers were being accepted by the police as useful and natural to this kind of police work. It does not suggest, however, that the researchers were being accepted and trusted as insiders—fellow police officers or family members—by these people.

While participating and observing in communes, Berger (1981) many times was asked to render expert advice or opinions about philosophy, sociology, family relations, and child rearing. He was requested to perform mundane tasks, such as providing transportation for people and supplies, and otherwise to participate in group activities. He (1981, pp. 215-17) even provided shelter to a fugitive member of the group and helped make possible his escape to Canada away from the FBI. Berger clearly became accepted and even trusted by the insiders, although there is no indication that they thought of him as being one of themselves.

Information collected from the standpoint of an outsider may be extremely valuable, yet there are important aspects of human existence that simply cannot be known except from the inside. The outsider role is most likely to be effective when the setting is fairly public and more or less accessible to anyone willing to spend sufficient time hanging around and observing to gain a sense of what transpires. Anderson (1978) initially participated in Jelly's Bar by hanging out. Cottle (1977) studied people's private lives simply by engaging them in public conversation.

For some research questions, it may not be necessary to undertake more involved roles. Not all investigators are capable of or well suited to assuming insider roles, or of becoming more intensely involved. Haaken and Adams (1983), for instance, described their participant observation of the self-help industry as genuine but restrained involvement. While acting like participants, they maintained personal and professional distance from lifespring training. Altheide and Johnson (1977) only pretended to be interested while participating in and observing an evangelical crusade.

There is no perfect participant strategy. Most human settings, however, do not give up the insiders' world of meaning and action except to a person willing to become a member. The deeper meanings of most forms of human existence are not displayed for outsiders. They are available primarily to people for whom these meanings constitute a way of life.

INSIDER ROLES

Participating as an insider requires the researcher to select from among the roles already available in the setting. Unlike the role of outside observer that is defined by the researcher and imposed by the setting, insider roles are provided by the setting. Douglas, Rasmussen, and Flanagan (1977) studied the nude beach scene, for example, by taking off their clothes and becoming nude beachers. Humphreys (1970) observed homosexual acts in public restrooms by way of the available role of lookout. Adler (1981) investigated momentum as an assistant basketball coach. I (1979, 1984) explored occult divinatory practice as a reader of the tarot. The performance of roles defined by the setting offers the distinct advantage of being in all ways a normal part of human interaction and, therefore, fairly unobtrusive.

The participant observer may perform a variety of roles over the course of a study. In investigating occultists, I (1979) initially assumed the readily available role of "seeker." My identification as someone looking for spiritual enlightenment was provided by insiders. I did not even realize that this definition had been applied to me for a considerable period of time. The seeker role provided me with an interesting status: I was able to perform the role covertly; I was seen as a natural part of the setting; I was able to observe and ask endless questions as a natural part of the role without raising people's suspicions; but I was still primarily an outsider.

After a period of seeking occult wisdom, it became difficult to sustain this role without providing further explanation of my presence. While seeking, I gradually made the transition to being defined by members of the setting as a "client" of occult practitioners. I was required to participate more actively in this role definition. As a client, I was on the threshold of the insiders' world of meaning. Unlike a seeker, I was permitted access to meanings and feelings that were less visible to the general public. Insiders demonstrated greater comfort in my presence; I was able to begin to establish trusting relationships; and I gradually came to be associated with particular people, groups, beliefs, practices, and even politics of the setting. I was not yet an insider but I had begun to achieve a status closer to that of an insider than an outsider.

The performance of multiple roles offers the distinct advantage of providing access to different standpoints and perspectives. The researcher gains a more comprehensive and accurate picture of what is happening simply by observing, but also by developing relationships with different people. These relationships, typically based on mutual interests, open up the setting for further participant observation.

In appropriating roles from the setting, you may experience problems managing self-concept, as Gold (1958, 1969) points out. Some roles are more readily assumed than others, depending on such factors as the extent of specialized expertise required and expectations insofar as interacting with other people. Some researchers find it easier and more enjoyable to perform roles defined by the setting than other investigators do. So long as the role to be performed is within the researcher's range of expertise and not in conflict with his or her other roles and self-concept, it is less likely to be problematic, although it may not necessarily be fun. Roles experienced as conflictual with your other roles and your concept of self are difficult to sustain for any length of time.

My role as seeker of occult wisdom, for instance, produced little conflict. I was sincerely interested in occult thinking and practices and I enjoyed most of these seeking experiences—I was free to explore ideas. My role as client of occult practitioners also was mostly free from conflict although I enjoyed being a client less than being a seeker. As a seeker I was relatively free from obligations. As a client, however, I was obligated to seek advice, behave as if I wanted and appreciated it, and act as if the advice really was very useful to me. My role as tarot card reader—a role providing full status as an insider—was the most conflictual. The most objectionable portion of the role was actually reading the cards, especially in public. Although I was sufficiently accomplished as a tarot card reader to pass as an insider among occultists, divination by cards presented a serious conflict with my identity as social scientist. I also was concerned about what consequences my divinatory activity might have for people receiving this advice.

Politics and multiple insider roles were remarkable in the nude beach study (Douglas and Rasmussen, with Flanagan, 1977). The nude beach was a hotly debated public issue: the police became involved; people were arrested; interest groups formed; and there was media coverage. As a nude beacher, Douglas was an insider to the thoughts and feelings of these people, including the politics of nudism. Douglas also participated, however, as a member of a property owners group near the beach. The property owners were among the most outspoken opponents of the nude beach. Hence, Douglas was in the unique position of being a participant observer from different *and* highly conflictual perspectives (see Douglas and Rasmussen, with Flanagan, 1977, pp. 193-222). He performed conflicting roles for a brief period of time. It would have been very difficult to sustain these conflicting roles without appropriate redefinition once rival parties knew of his participant involvements with the opposing political factions.

BECOMING THE PHENOMENON

Participant roles may be assumed nominally, or you may become more completely and intensely involved with the role performances. How the participant role is appropriated and performed depends on your own biography and interests, the role, the setting, and an almost endless variety of related factors. Some roles are experienced as demanding, other are not; some roles require little expertise, other roles require extensive training or expertise; some researchers become excellent role players, while other people never overcome the awkwardness that usually accompanies performance of a unfamiliar role. This may result in self-conflicts, poor role performances, and otherwise limit the ability to observe.

In everyday life, there is a fine line between who we pretend to be and who we are. Traditionally, participant observers have been warned about crossing this line. The participant observer who does this is said to have "gone native" or "become the phenomenon" (see Wax, 1971; Mehan and Wood, 1975; Douglas, 1976; Adler and Adler, 1987). When this happens, the researcher may be lost to the community of science perhaps never to return; the research may be contaminated by "subjectivity" and personal feelings; and the scientific identity of the researcher may be spoiled. Research "objectivity," in the traditional view, is not unlike virginity: Once lost, it cannot be recovered.

All of this seems rather ominous in the abstract. In some instances, these concerns may be justified. It is important that the researcher see clearly in the field, and be able to analyze and interpret observations critically. One of the principal advantages of participating while observing, however, is the possibility of experiencing the world of daily life as an insider. Sometimes this only can be accomplished by becoming the phenomenon and experiencing it existentially.

Membership is a privileged point of view, and ultimately it is acquired only by lived experience. Scott (1968) opportunistically exploited a membership role to describe the racing game in intimate detail. Likewise, Becker's (1963) participation as a jazz musician and marijuana smoker served to reveal these phenomena from a perspective of membership. Damrell's (1977, 1978) membership in two religious groups provided a unique perspective on these phenomena. Polsky's (1969) socially marginal existence opened the world of hustlers, beats, and other marginal people up to formal study. Irwin's (1970, 1980) early involvement in crime led to several studies of felons and prisons.

The difficulty I (1979) experienced with becoming a practitioner of tarot had nothing to do with overidentification with occultism or occultists. Just the opposite, I had difficulty in even temporarily suspending my scientific identity and viewpoint. Although I tried earnestly to become an occultist, I was unable to accomplish this awesome feat. Because of my commitment to science, I was unable to convince myself (although I did convince other people) that I was an occultist. Even after I was regarded by occultists as one of them, I found a scientific framework intruding into my thoughts and feelings, obscuring an occult perspective.

In spite of warnings to the contrary, participant observers in recent years have endeavored to become the phenomenon in order to achieve observational advantage. One of the most striking accounts of the successful employment of this strategy is Jules-Rosette's (1975) fieldwork with a native African fundamentalist-Christian group. Her report provides powerful confirmation of the observational advantage of this strategy with little indication that a loss of objectivity resulted (see, also, Krieger, 1985).

Jules-Rosette (1975) encountered the "Apostles" originally as a Western sociologist doing fieldwork on ritual practices in Africa. Sensing that she was not fully understanding the religious practices and rituals, Jules-Rosette began to participate more actively. Her participant involvements proved to be extremely valuable by way of opening up phenomena of study theretofore not apparent from the perspective of a nonparticipant. Eventually she became a fully participating member, and in the process she focused attention explicitly on membership as a topic of research. As a result of membership, Jules-Rosette is able to portray an amazingly vivid and richly detailed picture of the religious life from the insiders' viewpoint.

Although Jules-Rosette achieved the insiders' perspective to a much larger extent than most researchers, the fact that she returned to the community of science indicates that she never completely abandoned these commitments. She seems to have been able to suspend at least temporarily a scientific perspective for a religious one. Having internalized the insiders' beliefs, Jules-Rosette was able to employ it as a resource, along with notes and materials gathered in the field, turning a scientific framework back on for purposes of reflective, critical analysis.

As commonsense actors, people have the ability to manage multiple roles and selves even when the accompanying perspectives present logical and other contradictions (see Festinger, Riecken, and Schacter, 1956). Potentially conflicting beliefs may be separated into cognitive compartments. It is possible, even for extended periods, to hold multiple, contradictory beliefs, especially if the interactional situations where these perspectives are used can be kept separate. It also is possible to have internal dialogues between these perspectives. Most researchers become quite adept at turning on and off their analytic functions. You many times experience and interpret the world of daily life as a matter of common sense, while later turning on an analytic perspective to deal with a particular situation (see Zurcher, 1977).

Becoming the phenomenon is not necessary for successful participant observation and it can be problematic for the researcher's self-conception. Rambo (1987), for instance, constantly experienced conflict between being an exotic dancer and a sociology graduate student. Partly this was a consequence of Rambo having performed the dancer role in daily life prior to becoming a graduate student. Throughout her fieldwork, Rambo depended on me to talk out the analytic sociology of what she was doing and separate it from the intrusion of the dancer's perspective. During the period of her most intense field involvements, she found it necessary to talk over her experiences, oftentimes for several hours, prior to an evening of dancing. Although I constantly stressed to Rambo that further involvement as the phenomenon of interest was not essential to the study, after these sessions she made the decision to continue until *she* was satisfied that the strategy of becoming the phenomenon had been employed to optimal advantage.

Rambo's participant observation as the phenomenon of interest provided incredible access to the insider's experience of exotic dancing, especially the dancer's *feelings* and strategies for interacting with customers. Clearly her subjective involvement in this scene resulted in a much more accurate (objective) description of the dancing experience than would have been possible by any other strategy. I was able to provide a perspective on Rambo's experiences from the standpoint of an outsider. She did experience difficulty, however, with conflict between her self-conceptions as a dancer and as a graduate student. For what was a fairly short period of time (less than two months), she was able to treat these difficulties by having people talk over and analyze her experiences sociologically.

In short, then, becoming the phenomenon is a participant observational strategy for penetrating to and gaining direct experience of a form of human life. It is an objective approach insofar as it results in the accurate, detailed description of the insiders' experience of life. In carrying out this strategy, it is important that the researcher be able to switch back and forth between the insiders' perspective and an analytic framework. This may be facilitated by talking over field experiences with colleagues. Like all scientific findings, the results of participant observation are open to public, peer review. Participant observation, unlike many approaches, requires that the researcher carefully and very specifically describe how methods of investigation were used to produce particular results.

TEAM STRATEGIES AND USING ASSISTANTS

A single researcher, even if she or he is able to perform multiple and varied participant roles, fundamentally is limited in terms of the perspectives on the insiders' world that may be assumed. There are certain built-in limitations to what may be observed and experienced by the solo researcher. The participant observer's status, such as gender, ethnicity, and age, is difficult to alter or change for more than very brief encounters. Social status, however, very often has importance for observation (see Wax, 1979).

Access to human meanings and situations, especially to the meanings of insiders, frequently depends on social location and status. Activities involving gender, for instance, may be difficult to observe except from the perspective of people of the appropriate gender. Teams of participant observers or the use of trained assistants may be extremely valuable and even necessary if high-quality data are to be collected.

Team participant observation does not differ significantly from studies conducted by a single researcher, except that teams are able to divide labor in such a way as to gain access to multiple perspectives. Team strategies offer the advantage that research is not entirely dependent on the personal interests and interpersonal skills of one participant observer. Members of a team generally are able to sustain constant communication about emergent findings and problems. Haaken and Adams (1983), for instance, made use of their training in psychiatry and sociology to gain different perspectives on lifespring training.

Douglas, Rasmussen, and Flanagan's (1977) study of the nude beach further illustrates the effective use of a team research strategy. Each of the researchers was able to provide a slightly different existential perspective on beach life. Douglas's perspective was influenced by his location as a middle-aged, married university professor and home owner near the beach. Rasmussen's location was very different: He was younger, single, and a graduate student. Flanagan provided still another perspective as a youthful female graduate student. Neither Rasmussen nor Flanagan, due to their status characteristics, was able to provide the perspective Douglas brought to the study, especially sociological expertise and the view of local home owners. Neither Douglas nor Rasmussen, on the other hand, was able to provide a view of the nude beach from a woman's standpoint. Age and marital status provided differences between the views of Douglas and Rasmussen.

A unique team strategy is reported by Feldman, Agar, and Beschner (1979). Four participant observers—two males and two females—investigated the use of angel dust (phencyclidine) in different areas of the United States. All of them were studying phencyclidine use when they decided to collaborate because of urgent public health concerns. During a very brief three-and-one-half month period, the researchers exploited their existing positions as participant observers and collectively addressed basic questions of public health. The multiple differences in perspective—based on gender, regional location, theoretical focus, and so on—greatly contributed to confidence that these findings would be useful in developing social policy and specific treatment approaches to this social problem.

Like team research strategies, the use of research assistants may enhance the breadth and quality of data by providing multiple perspectives. Unlike team research, assistants generally are employed for fairly specific purposes. At least two general categories of research assistants may be distinguished. First, because many researchers also teach at institutions of higher education, students frequently are employed for particular aspects of a research project. Second, participant observers encounter people in the field who may be recruited as assistants.

Student assistants differ in interests, training, and abilities. Undergraduate students are particularly appropriate for specific tasks. I employed undergraduate students with little research experience for the purpose of collecting tarot card readings. With very little instruction, I was able to send assistants to a tarot card reader. They frequently were able to tape-record the reading for me and they were requested to keep field notes. I later debriefed them for the purposes of gathering further information and teaching them participant observation.

Zimmerman and Weider (1977) employed undergraduate students even more extensively. They were interested in the youth drug culture, especially the jargon people used to construct and make sense of this form of life. Students who also were involved in the drug subculture were especially appropriate for this mission. Zimmerman and Weider had the students keep field notes of their experiences, and they conducted debriefing and interviewing sessions with the students.

Natives sometimes make not only outstanding informants but also excellent field-workers. Unlike the researcher from outside the social world, insiders already are located within the environment. Like with student assistants, what one can expect native field-workers to accomplish greatly depends on the individual. Under most circumstances, the use of assistants from within a setting is best restricted to particular tasks supervised by the professional researcher. Participant observers, however, even in settings where one would not expect to find colleagues, have reported encountering and employing people who all but became fully trusted coworkers. Like especially talented natives, graduate students many times may be depended upon to assume major responsibilities.

Gallimeier (1987, forthcoming), for instance, recruited a key informant from among professional hockey players to assist with data collection. The player, "Crawdaddy," was well suited to this task because of his undergraduate degree in sociology. Crawdaddy kept a chronologically organized diary and he was subject to lengthy, detailed, and probing interviews by Gallimeier (following the recommendations of Zimmerman and Weider, 1977).

SUMMARY

Principles and strategies for participating in everyday life settings have been discussed and illustrated in this chapter. The physical and social location of the participant observer determines what may be experienced and observed. The participant role may be as a complete outsider, a complete insider, or various ranges between the outside and inside of a phenomenon of interest. Becoming the phenomenon is a unique strategy for experiencing the world from the standpoint of a complete insider. In participating, you should be sensitive to ethical issues, politics, and complications regarding your self-concept. Participation may involve a single researcher or a research team. Teams of participant observers offer distinctive advantages, including the possibility of gathering information from multiple perspectives.

EXERCISES

1. Suppose you are a participant in some form of daily life (such as a senior high school prom). Identify different social locations (such as member of the band, female student, male student, mother, father, and so on) at this event. Describe and discuss how different locations would result in different perspectives about the event. Feel free to provide your own example.

2. You have been recruited to do a study of high school dropouts (or drug users or police). How might this topic be approached using the participant observational study of becoming the phenomenon? Is this strategy appropriate? Why or why not? What problems might be encountered in carrying out this form of participant observation? Discuss the advantages and disadvantages of this strategy.

3. Using one of the topics mentioned above, compare and contrast how it might be studied by a single participant observer and by a team of researchers. What are the advantages or disadvantages between solo and team approaches to participant observation?

4. Select an instance of participant observation from the literature. Critically analyze this example in terms of the location of the researcher, the participant role or roles used, ethics, and politics. Was this use of participant observation effective? Why or why not?

5

Developing and Sustaining
Field Relationships

Principles and methods for developing and sustaining relationships characterized by trust, cooperation, rapport, and friendship are discussed and illustrated in this chapter. Field relationships depend on negotiation, reciprocity, and exchange, and they raise important political and ethical issues. Obstacles to satisfactory relations between the participant observer and people in everyday life situations are described. Strategies for dealing with problematic relations in the field are discussed and illustrated.

TRUST AND COOPERATION

Lies, exaggerations, intentional and unintentional deceptions (including self-deception), interpersonal front work or pretenses, lack of or severely limited knowledge, misunderstandings, and the like all present serious problems to the collection of accurate and dependable information (Douglas, 1976, 1985). The quality of data is improved when the participant observer establishes and sustains trusting and cooperative relationships with people in the field (Johnson, 1975). Knowledge of a person's social identity (biography, status, roles, and the like) provides grounds for developing trust and cooperation, as well as for evaluating the information they furnish. In judging the truthfulness of what people tell you, it is important to ask: How do they know this? Do they have an interest in this information? Is the account consistent with their experience? Is the information otherwise believable? Can the data be confirmed or disconfirmed by other people? Commonsense knowledge provides guidelines for making these judgments. Most of us, in other words, evaluate people and information in everyday life. The participant observer seeks to refine and cultivate existing interpersonal skills for research purposes.

Trust and cooperation are not absolute, rather they are matters of degree. Your relationships with people in daily life are more or less cooperative and more or less trusting. During field study, you most likely will develop very trusting, even intimate relationships and friendships with a few people; maintain good, but less intimate relations with other folks; and develop casual acquaintances involving limited trust and cooperation with still others. Trust and cooperation are interactional. Insiders will find you *more or less* interesting, likable, friendly, and trustworthy. As a participant observer, you may deliberately manage your self-presentation so as to encourage (or discourage) the development of particular relationships.

Trust and cooperation among people are influenced greatly by particular circumstances and situations. You should deliberately cultivate skill in reading or interpreting social interactional situations. A growing relationship of trust with an informant, for instance, may be spoiled if you fail to notice that she or he is uncomfortable talking because of the situation itself or the people present in a particular situation. Accurate and dependable information depends on the kind and degree of relationships you are able to establish with people, and the situations wherein the interactions transpire.

Human relations based on trust and cooperation are dynamic and constantly problematic conditions of social life. They require ongoing attention to be sustained. Trust and cooperation may be withdrawn at any time. The participant observer must be prepared to evaluate when there is "sufficient" trust and cooperation to support the collection of accurate and dependable information (Johnson, 1975). In other words, you need to ask yourself if a relationship of trust and cooperation has been established sufficiently for you to be able to depend on the information gleaned. There are few absolute rules for making this decision, yet most of us have a commonsense ability to make these judgments. Does the informant, for instance, tell you more than would be told to a stranger? Do you feel comfortable interacting with one another? Can you laugh and joke together? How much do you know about this person and their social history?

Trusting and cooperative relationships among the participant observer and the insiders in the field setting, in short, are necessary for unobstructed access to the daily existence of insiders and for accurate, dependable, high-quality information about their world. Trust and cooperation are matters of degree. The participant observer should seek to maximize cooperation and trust with at least a few key people in the field setting. Trust and cooperation constantly are problematic and depend on ongoing interactional work in concrete situations. You will have to decide while in the field and doing fieldwork when there is sufficient cooperation and trust to support truth claims. You, in other words, constantly must interpret and evaluate information in terms of who is providing it, the degree and character of the relationship involved, and the situations and settings in which you interact with insiders. Blau's (1964) failure to establish sufficient rapport with informants before conducting formal interviews resulted in his distrust.

RECIPROCITY AND EXCHANGE

Field relations involve negotiation and exchange between the participant observer and insiders (see Blau, 1964; Whyte, 1984). Although some transactions may involve money or material items, the medium of exchange most likely will be nonmaterial and symbolic. Whether or not people are self-consciously aware of it, all parties to a relationship expect something or some value from these interactions. Clearly, you want something: access to the insiders' way of life, the opportunity to participate and observe, and information.

Insiders may or may not have anything to gain, individually or collectively, by trusting and cooperating with you. They commonly do not share the researcher's conviction that knowledge resulting from research will be valuable in some way to members of the setting. In seeking to establish cooperative relations with Vietnam veterans in order to describe the problems they face daily (due to combat experience), I constantly have been forced to address this question. One of the first questions they put to me is "What's in this for you?" they also ask: "Why should I cooperate with this research?" Or "What's in this for me?"

What do you have to offer people in exchange for trust, cooperation, information, and friendship? This is an important political and ethical issue that defies simple solution. Because of previous experience, Vietnam veterans, for instance, generally are not persuaded by the argument that research may result in knowledge useful for treating the problems of their daily existence. Most of them are not in the least awed by any would-be prestige of science or scientist, and their experience supports more than a healthy skepticism of would-be "do-gooders" and service organizations. I have found it advisable to be direct and extremely candid with these men. I tell them precisely what I expect to gain from the research (publications, prestige, knowledge), and that while I sincerely hope it will be useful to people like themselves, I do not anticipate that my research will change their lives significantly. I promise them nothing beyond honesty, respect, and the possibility of mutual friendship. Because of many veterans' profound cynicism and their distrust of people's self-interested motives, this boldly honest approach commonly is disarming and successful where a less candid, more pretentious approach would fail entirely.

Veterans also are persuaded by the claim that because participant observation is committed to describing reality from the insiders' perspective it is less exploitative than many forms of human studies. An understanding of particular forms of life from the insiders' standpoint does have a value in and of itself, even if it provides no guarantee against subsequent abuse or exploitation. Because the participant observer must interact directly with insiders, it is more difficult to ignore their thoughts, feelings, and interests. Direct participant involvement has a humanizing potential, then, generally lacking in studies conducted from a greater distance from the people whose lives are affected. In the final analysis, you must be prepared to defend, publicly if necessary, the justice and ethics of relations with people in the field.

Morally responsible participant observation requires that you be alert for ways of providing something of value in exchange for what you get from insiders. The least satisfactory medium of exchange is money. Douglas (1976, p. 141) bluntly observes that "if one pays a lover for her services, one prostitutes her; and he gets phoney love, mere self-presentations, in return." In some situations, money may be an appropriate form of exchange, but be aware that it defines the relationship as a business and on this basis influences what is being exchanged. It generally is appropriate, for instance, to pay people for assisting with the collection of information or to offer money or something else of value as a gift in reward for assistance. Notice, however, that within this culture friends exchange favors and items of value, including money, but they rarely trade these same items for friendship without negative consequences.

You will discover a wide variety of ways to solidify cooperation and trust by engaging in fair exchanges that do not involve money. Exchanges involving praise, compliments, and the performing of favors generally are even more powerful than money in cementing cooperative and trusting relationships (Blau, 1964). Friendship indeed very often is based on little more than acknowledgment of common interests and mutual respect. Though mostly symbolic, *respect* is a very powerful and valuable medium to give or exchange with another person. My most trusted informants on occultism, for instance, appreciated my respect and friendship much more than any money I might have offered them (see Jorgensen, 1979). Ellis (1986) likewise repaid the fisher folk she studied with favors, small gifts, and, most important, a sincere interest in and respect for them and their way of life.

Under exceptionally difficult circumstances, Adler (1985) went beyond the ordinary call of duty in developing exchange relations with upper-level drug dealers. By doing favors, such as baby-sitting dealers' children, offering use of her phone and car, and providing members of this drug subculture with a place to crash, Adler was able to gain acceptance and establish unusual rapport. In one instance, she helped a dealer with legal services and related matters after he was arrested, convicted, and imprisoned for dealing. After the dealer's release from jail, he lived with the Adlers for a period of seven months while becoming reintegrated into daily life. This dealer became more than a cooperative and trusted informant, he became one of the Adlers' *friends*.

STRATEGIES FOR DEVELOPING RELATIONS

The participant observer initially encounters people in the field as strangers. These people, similarly, experience you as a unfamiliar person even if they have some knowledge of your actual or assumed identity. The responses of insiders may range from hatred, hostility, and dislike to indifference, toleration, guarded cooperation, friendship, and even great warmth and intimacy. You, likewise, may experience an entire range of emotions—hatred, dislike, fear, indifference, toleration, friendship, love—with regard to people within the setting generally and/or with particular individuals.

Gaining Acceptance

From the very first encounter with insiders, a central objective should be to gain some degree of acceptance from them. You do not need to be liked or loved as a participant observer, but it is necessary that natives do not find your presence too objectionable or intolerable. Once you are accepted without major objection or reservation, there will be plenty of time to develop closer relations. Initially, you are well advised to be as unobtrusive as possible in the setting. Anything likely to call attention to yourself generally should be avoided.

It is best at the outset to blend into the setting and particular situations, carefully watching and listening to what transpires, so as to become familiar with the scene and the insiders' way of daily life. It is best not to be outspoken; to respond to people as is deemed appropriate for the situation; and otherwise to attempt to be present but in no way obtrusive. The aim of gaining acceptance requires that you dress and behave in such a way as not to call attention to yourself. To do this, you must interpret the situation and setting where you are involved to discover appropriate ways of fitting in. Gaining acceptance is like learning a different culture or subculture. This phase of participant observation sometimes is called "learning the ropes" (see Shaffir, Stebbins, and Turowetz, 1980).

The covert participant observer should adopt a role and demeanor appropriate to the passive strategy of being unobtrusive. Under most circumstances, it will be sufficient to conform to whatever expectations insiders hold for this role. If possible, leave questions about who you are and what you are doing there ambiguous; yet do provide sufficient information to avoid creating undue interest in your presence. Your objective is to become socialized and accepted into the host culture as an ordinary participant.

The overt participant observer faces a different situation. Because some people, even if not all, have at least limited knowledge of the research, further explanation frequently is necessary. Members of the setting generally will have questions about exactly what you hope to find, what it is you will be doing, and whether or not or in what ways they may be involved in the research. It is not at all uncommon for people to form largely mistaken impressions of the research and its consequences for them. Perhaps the most important initial task of the overt participant in seeking to establish field relations is to overcome peoples' prejudices about you and the research.

In participating overtly, it is important to deal with peoples' questions openly and directly. You need to *normalize* your presence in the field. Depending on the setting, you may be able to gain cooperation because people think that research is valuable. Natives not uncommonly will regard their relationships with you as intrinsically valuable or as a source of personal prestige and power. You are not a member and consequently should not behave as one. Insiders do not expect a researcher to act as a member, and they may be offended if you do (see Whyte, 1984).

Insiders may need to be reassured that you will not harm them or their interests. It may be useful to emphasize that their cooperation is *voluntary*, their identity will remain *anonymous*, and any information they provide will be *confidential*. It may help to discuss the research plan with people in the field in order to dispel possible misconceptions and gain their acceptance, although it is not necessary to reveal the subtleties of the research. Exactly where the research will lead may not be entirely clear because basic questions still are emerging. Highly technical accounts of the research generally are not necessary or desirable. It usually is sufficient to provide a general, though concise overview of the study, and then answer insiders' questions.

Toleration and acceptance by insiders may be gained quickly and easily, or it may require a concerted effort over longer periods of time. While some people may be accepting, other people may be reserved or even worse. Once granted, acceptance may be revoked at any time. You should be alert for signs of toleration and acceptance. These signs may be subtle: body language and gestures, lack of objections by members of the setting to participant involvement, or merely a feeling on your part that interaction is routine and normal. Or your acceptance may be more obvious, as when people express their interest in you or friendship.

Toleration and acceptance generally require moral neutrality regarding members' beliefs, values, and activities (see Whyte, 1955). Insiders may request or even require that you become morally accepting of or committed to their way of life. How well you pass these tests generally determines subsequent relationships. In studying a fundamentalist Christian school, for instance, Peshkin (1986) was tested repeatedly by efforts to convert him—in spite of, or maybe even because of, the fact that he is Jewish. Peshkin passed these tests in that members of the school continued to tolerate his presence and even cooperated with him. Signs of toleration and acceptance are very important. They suggest that you have been examined and evaluated by insiders and found to be *morally* worthy company (Johnson, 1975). Acceptance, in other words, is a moral judgment by insiders about you. Acceptance does not necessarily indicate that insiders judge you to be morally equal to themselves.

Developing Rapport

Genuine rapport with insiders requires more than mere toleration and nominal acceptance (see Hunt, 1984). It requires that peoples' feelings toward one another are quite positive. Rapport commonly is related to your ability to demonstrate a degree of accomplishment with the host culture and willingness to give something of yourself in interacting with members. The process of establishing rapport with people in the field very much resembles how we go about making friends in everyday life, except that it is more deliberate and self-conscious. A high degree of rapport with natives generally requires extensive and intensive ordinary participation in their way of life.

Rapport does not necessarily mean that you always agree with insiders or conform to their expectations. Gordon (1987) successfully developed rapport with Jesus People in spite of open disagreements with them over matters of belief. This strategy of "empathetic disagreements" also enabled Gordon to reduce the stressfulness of participant observation.

People with whom you have previously exchanged eye contact, gestures, or conversation provide places to begin seeking rapport. By engaging people in conversation, you will discover mutual interests. Participating with people under the ordinary conditions of their existence serves to build common experiences and rapport. Even simple expressions of concern for other people frequently lead them to open up and tell you of their interests, activities, and experiences. Being caring, sympathetic, and willing to listen to insiders commonly leads to rapport and friendship.

The perception of social barriers and distance among people may create obstacles to subsequent relations. Insiders, for instance, may judge your social worth as greater or less than their own and interact with you accordingly. Age, ethnicity, and gender are grounds for much social distance. Rapport requires that these distances be bridged. Corsaro (1985), for instance, encountered a serious rapport problem in studying preschool children. He began participating by hanging around the school, nominally engaging in school activities, such as helping the children getting ready to leave for home. Corsaro became a more or less routine, nonthreatening feature of the school. Eventually the children began to take notice of Corsaro and engage him in conversation.

With signs of toleration and acceptance by the children, Corsaro gradually entered into play activities without disrupting them—providing further indication that rapport was being established. The children began calling him "Big Bill," acknowledging with this nickname a high degree of acceptance. By choosing this name, the children also acknowledged differences between Big Bill and themselves, as well as certain differences between Corsaro and the teachers. A key to

Corsaro's rapport was direct participant involvement with the children. Most important, Big Bill, unlike other adults, did not exercise authority over them. Eventually, the children accepted Big Bill into their activities, insisting that he sit with them, play with them, and be included at their birthday parties more or less as a peer. Corsaro consequently was able to overcome a social distance as great as any likely to be encountered.

The participant observer's biography may be used to overcome social distance. Discovering and sharing common life experiences are effective in generating sympathetic understanding and social bonds among people. Similarities in age, current or former residential locations, military service, religion, marital status or history, employment, hobbies, and so on frequently are bases for emergent rapport. The development of genuine rapport with people, perhaps leading to friendship, is most effective when sincere. Participant observers, however, have been known to invent, imagine, or adapt biographical experience to suit a particular purpose or occasion for securing rapport (Johnson, 1975).

Self-revelation is a very effective commonsense strategy for generating rapport. By this strategy, you tell someone a detail about yourself, usually something you would not tell just anyone, such as a personal secret. Self-revelations commonly are shared with the warning that the information must remain secret. The sharing of this information creates common experience that ostensibly is special or based on a special relationship. It represents a gift, a confidence, a sign of respect and trust for the person to whom you reveal yourself. And like all gifts, it creates an obligation for the receiver to exchange something—such as a self-revelation of their own—of equal or greater value with you.

Although one's deepest and darkest secrets may be reserved for very close intimates, people not uncommonly make surprisingly revealing self-disclosures to people they hardly know. Kotarba (1980), for instance, found that strangers openly revealed intimate details about their health and illnesses. This is not especially surprising, however, given that one's secrets may be safer with a complete stranger whom you probably will never see again, than with the best friend who is part of your daily life. The strategy of self-revelation, in any case, is an effective tool for developing rapport in the field because it creates the sense of common, even intimate, experience between people.

Perhaps the most effective general strategy for solidifying sympathetic field relations is to engage in joint activities. By participating together, people create shared experiences. Shared experience serves as the cement for feelings of mutual interrelationship and friendship. Unusual experiences, ones characterized by a high degree of emotion, are especially effective in producing solidarity. War veterans, prisoners, victims of crime, and the like commonly enjoy instant rapport with one another due to the intensity of past experiences they share in common. Mutual participation in slightly deviant or illegal activities tends to be very conducive to a sense of rapport and friendship. Similar feelings are created by ethnic and religious identities as well as by identities derived from other group memberships. These activities serve to mark the boundaries between insiders and outsiders, creating distinctive "we" feelings and solidarity.

STRATEGIES FOR OVERCOMING OBSTACLES

Participant observers may expect to encounter people and situations that are resistant to establishing and maintaining satisfactory field relations. Some people may remain cool, cold, distrustful, hostile, and even feel hatred for the participant observer. These people and situations, in turn, provoke emotional responses from the participant observer. Social life is political: Friendly and trusting relations with one set of insiders may result in unfriendly and hostile relations on the part of other people in the setting. You should be prepared to recognize and deal with these people and situations.

Difficulties with People and Settings

Hostile, conflictual, distrustful, unfriendly relationships with people create serious barriers to gathering accurate and dependable information. A lack of cooperation, however, sometimes can be turned to advantage. It is at times effective to engage people directly in conversation about the reasons for their unfriendly or hostile reaction to you. Simply permitting them to express these feelings may result in subsequent cooperation, and it may be possible to counter a misconception or provide reasons for their cooperation. Even if you are not successful, the information provided by uncooperative insiders may be valuable for gaining insight into their world.

Peshkin's (1986) initial efforts to locate a setting appropriate for the study of fundamentalist Christian schools, for instance, was met with tremendous hostility by ministers and school authorities. He was denied access repeatedly, yet these experiences were informative. Because of these difficulties, Peshkin developed a greater understanding for the boundaries between insiders and outsiders, as well as specific objections by fundamentalists to his research.

Every human situation is a political one. Insiders are self-invested in what happens, and inevitably there are ongoing conflicts, struggles for power, and forceful disagreements. Trusting relationships with some people in this context very well may preclude trusting relationships with other people, factions, networks, and groups. In observing networks of occultists, for instance, I (1979) developed close relationships with several people long before I became fully aware of the major factions and political conflicts present in the esoteric community. Partly because I cultivated many casual relationships with people from all the major segments (quite by accident) and partly because their definition of me as belonging to this or that group or faction occurred gradually, this created few problems until very late in the research.

Eventually, however, I was involved directly in a bitter dispute among conflicting factions. I did not participate in a psychic fair sponsored by one of the spiritual groups in the community, contrary to the expectation (mistaken, I think) of the group's minister. I attempted to explain the misunderstanding and otherwise smooth out and diffuse the conflict through a series of telephone conversations. The minister, however, already had concluded that my involvement in the community reflected the "materialistic" values of a rival political segment, and he thereby denounced me, my friends, and our commitment to occultism. I attempted, somewhat feebly, to remedy this problem on subsequent occasions, to no avail. The minister and members close to these political interests in the community were sure about where I fit into the local occult scene. Consequently, never again during the project was I able to interact with these people on a friendly basis. Access to their activities also was denied. This episode was personally traumatizing, and extremely problematic for me. It nevertheless was invaluable in confirming the emergent picture I was developing of networks, segments, and politics in this community of occultists.

The Participant Observer's Self

Relations with people in the field are interconnected with the participant observer's self-concept. How you imagine yourself influences how you relate with insiders, and in turn this influences people's reactions to you. Your self-concept affects participant role performances, data collection, and other aspects of the research.

Upon entering the field, the participant observer tends to be interested, curious, and excited about doing research. These feelings frequently are mixed with fear or apprehension. Participation may lead to disappointment, disillusionment, disenchantment, dislike, and even hatred for particular situations, people, or even for the entire research setting. The marginality resulting from overt participation may be difficult to endure over any lengthy period of time. Intense covert participation may be even more demanding because it requires that you perform a membership role, and perhaps sustain insincere fronts and pretenses.

No matter how carefully you insulate yourself from the daily realities of fieldwork, it is unrealistic to think that you will not be affected. Wiley (1987), for instance, experienced a certain disorientation or confusion in moving between the mental health settings she participated in and the world of her ordinary daily life. It is important to anticipate these feelings and their consequences. Participant observers find it very useful to have professional colleagues or close friends willing to listen to accounts of daily experiences, and especially problem situations. You may find it useful to confront your feelings by recording and discussing them in your notes. Later, you consequently will be able to review these materials and evaluate how these feelings influenced you and the study (see Johnson, 1975).

SUMMARY

Developing and sustaining relationships with insiders in the field is crucial to gathering accurate and dependable information. This process is not unlike being socialized into a way of life. It involves hanging around, listening, watching, and otherwise learning the ropes. Establishing and maintaining relationships based on trust and cooperation depend on the deliberate use of commonsense abilities and strategies for gaining rapport and making friends with people within particular situations. These strategies include being open and willing to listen to other people, seeking out common interests, self-disclosures, and establishing common experiences through joint participation. Field relationships involve exchanges of material and nonmaterial items among people. The participant observer may offer money, services, or friendship in exchange for the cooperation of insiders.

Not all insiders or situations will react favorably to your efforts to develop cooperative relations. Negative responses to the participant observer, however, sometimes provide useful information. The participant observer should be alert to possible political complications and conscious of the ethics of participation. It is important that there be a defensible rate of exchange between insiders and the researcher. Participant observation generally is influenced by and influences your own self-image. Potential problems related to self-concept and feelings may be treated by talking them out with associates and friends, recording and discussing them in your notes, and reflecting on these matters once you have gained distance from them.

EXERCISES

1. Select an article or book (use the journals listed in the first exercise or the references at the end of the book) representing participant observation. Discuss the procedures used by the researcher to develop and sustain field relationships. To what extent were these relationships cooperative and trusting? How did this influence the data collected? Did the researcher encounter particular problems in developing and sustaining relationships? If so, how were these problems handled?

2. Briefly review your personal relationships. To what extent do these relationships involve different degrees of trust and cooperation? Discuss how they are based on exchange. List some of the ways that your commonsense abilities to interact with people might be useful in participant observation.

3. Identify a setting for participant observation (like a school, hospital, church, bank, corporation) and discuss how you might go about developing and sustaining cooperative and trusting relationships with insiders of this setting. What kinds of problems might you encounter? What political and ethical issues would be involved? How would you deal with them?

4. A lack of rapport with people is a serious obstacle to data collection. Less serious, but sometimes problematic, is becoming deeply involved with insiders, or what is called "overrapport." Outline and discuss how a lack of rapport or overrapport might influence the findings of participant observation. Use illustrations from your personal relationships if needed. Which of these situations do you think is more serious? How would you deal with them?

6

Observing and Gathering Information

This chapter describes and illustrates strategies for observing and collecting information. Observing while participating is a primary method of gathering information. Participant observers also engage in interviewing and sometimes employ questionnaires. Human communications, especially documents, artifacts, and personal experience, provide further sources of information.

OBSERVING WHILE PARTICIPATING

Observation begins the moment the participant observer makes contact with a potential field setting. Aside from collecting information, the basic goal of these largely unfocused initial observations is to become increasingly familiar with the insiders' world so as to refine and focus subsequent observation and data collection. It is extremely important that you record these observations as immediately as possible and with the greatest possible detail because never again will you experience the setting as so utterly unfamiliar.

Unfocused Observations

It is important at the outset of inquiry to remain open to the unexpected, even if you have previous experience in the setting. Previous experience and knowledge may be inappropriate, somewhat slanted, or simply incorrect. If previous experience and knowledge is confirmed by direct observation, you will have more powerful, empirical evidence of these facts. If not, misunderstandings may be corrected and you will be in a position to make new discoveries.

Upon entering a new situation or setting, survey the general features of this human landscape. This is largely a matter of becoming self-conscious and disciplined with respect to what most of us do anyway in everyday life. Look for the main features of the physical land space: What kind of space (or building) is this? Is it typical of other buildings of this sort? Or is it somehow unusual? How is the space organized? Is the space usual or somehow strange? What kinds of things are in this space or building? How is the space organized? By answering questions of this sort, you should be able to describe the physical contours of some space or building, thereby forming impressions about it.

The same strategy is useful for becoming familiar with and gathering information about people and events. How many people are there? Attend closely to how they look: What are their ages? genders? ethnicity? How are they attired? Can you see signs of social status and rank or visibly discern whether or not people are coupled or married? Is there anything unusual or striking about these people?

How are the people in this space arranged or organized? Can you on this or some other observational basis discern connections or relationships among those present? Are people, for instance, arranged in couples? in cliques? in family groups? or in some other recognizable patterns (such as age or gender)? What are people doing? What kind of gathering is it? Is this state of affairs somehow typical? Or is it discernibly unusual in some way? What feelings do you get in this setting? Do you have a sense of things that you are unable exactly to account for observationally?

These questions clearly do not exhaust the issues you should address. They provide a general model, however, of a strategy for asking questions about a wide variety of matters that may be of possible interest in human settings. Remember that, aside from gathering information, a basic aim of preliminary observations is to become familiar with the setting.

Your direct participation in the setting should be limited until a preliminary impression of what is happening begins to emerge. Ideally, you would be present without anyone knowing it. The key to this strategy, however, is to quickly achieve a "feel" for the setting and then attempt to fit in, being as unobtrusive as possible. This may, of course, require some involvement on your part. To refuse answering direct questions, for instance, would be considered rude in most situations and make you stand out. When in doubt about how to behave, it generally is wise to conform to patterns of behavior pertinent to your *role* in the setting.

More Focused Observation

Once you are more familiar with the setting, it is appropriate to begin focusing observational attention on matters of specific interest. What you select to concentrate observation on should be derived from the emerging problem and issues of study. The strategy of focusing your observational field is to begin with the widest possible range of phenomena, gradually limiting your attention to particular phenomena. What, in other words, can you learn about this phenomenon simply by looking and listening? What you have learned then may be used to address more specific interests. In other words, previous observations should result in an interest in phenomena that you would like to observe in more specific, systematic detail. This process of observing, analyzing, refocusing, and observing again may be repeated over and over again as you explore and refine emerging problems and questions for inquiry. At the same time, of course, you are engaged in the collection and recording of potentially important facts.

My (1979) initial interest in occultism, it may be recalled, was in divinatory practices. In trying to locate a setting for this study, I came across book and supply stores specializing in the occult. Observation of these establishments resulted in lists of individuals and groups as well as references to a local "community" of occultists. Observing what this community involved resulted in a conception of a diffuse cultic milieu and social networks of groups and practitioners. Observation of these networks led to a notion of the division of this community into segments. Observation of these segments resulted in the identification of inclusive individuals and groups. Observation of these groups and individuals led to a description of distinctive beliefs, practices, and ideologies. In short, then, preliminary observations lead to additional matters of possible interest. Focusing on these matters results in the identification of still other phenomena for observation, and so on in what may seem like a never-ending cycle of observation, analysis, redefinition, and observation.

More focused observations should lead to greater involvement with people in the setting and specifically to informal conversations and casual questioning. By this point in most settings you already will be interacting with people to some extent. This interaction may be largely a matter of performing an assumed role and otherwise getting on as a would-be insider, but almost every occasion for interaction also is an opportunity to learn something, generally or specifically, about the study problem and questions. Inevitably, this tends to be extremely awkward at first. You probably will experience some difficulty attending to the performance of participant roles while at the same time engaging in activities like casually raising questions. To the extent that you are able to become comfortable with the participant role, thereby routinizing its performance, it will become easier to concentrate attention on asking specific questions.

As with observing generally, there is a certain art to asking questions and engaging people in casual conversations (see Douglas, 1985). There are several keys to asking questions. Unobtrusive, casual questioning very much resembles ordinary, everyday life conversation (see Cottle, 1977). Your questions should be related to topics already introduced or suggested by the situation, context, and what has transpired therein. Good conversationalists generally do not violate the rules for introducing or taking up a topic, and they conform to similar rules for taking turns and recognizing the implicit right of other people to join the conversation. Certain topics, depending on the social context, are legitimate for discussion, while other topics and questions are inappropriate or even rude, impolite, or offensive in a given situation.

Questions about one's sexual behavior or preferences, for instance, tend to be legitimate only between people who already are intimate friends, and even then specific questions may be risky. Good conversationalists also know that license to ask questions and otherwise participate in the conversation frequently is earned by demonstrating a willingness, even an eagerness to listen to what other people have to say. Listening is the main feature of collecting data by casual conversations. Questioning, in this context, is most appropriate for getting people to continue talking, to suggest further discussion of a particular issue, or to direct conversation very carefully toward a topic of special interest.

INTERVIEWING

Interviewing refers to a range of strategies for more formally asking questions. As the problem and issue for study become increasingly clear and well defined, participant observers find it appropriate to use interviewing methods. Highly formal interviews may conform to a precise schedule of questions or take the form of a structured questionnaire.

Asking Questions

Asking questions is an artful activity. The initial questions you ask probably will be simple requests for general information raised as part of ordinary conversation. While such impromptu questioning is invaluable for generally learning about the insiders' world of thought, feeling, and action, eventually you will find a need for more systematically seeking answers to study issues and problems.

To question people directly requires that you provide good reasons for doing so in most situations. You may be able to assume a natural role available in the setting while conducting interviews, but more than likely you will have to justify formal interviewing explicitly by acknowledging your research interests. Explanation of the research should be general. It is sufficient in most instances to say something like "I'm doing a study of so and so." If further information is needed, people will request it. What else you need to say will depend on the nature of their questions. Tell them enough to answer their queries, diffuse suspicions or potentially disrupting misconceptions, and gain their confidence. It usually is better to say too little rather than too much. This activity should be as unobtrusive as possible. Saying too much may lead to misunderstandings, apprehensiveness, suspicion, and the like on the part of insiders or otherwise intrude into the interviewing process. The more this happens, the less certain it is that what people tell you represents their true thoughts and feelings.

Exactly what questions you ask depend on your study problem. There are a general range of issues pertinent to most human studies and most model strategies. Spradley (1979), talking specifically about the "ethnographic interview," outlines several types of questions and principles for asking them. *Descriptive questions* are general requests for information about people, places, events, and so on (Spradley, 1979, pp. 78-91). Descriptive questions explore the general contours of some matter in fairly comprehensive detail. These kinds of questions commonly take the form: "tell me about x, y, or z, I am interested in what you think about this"; "tell me what you do when you engage in this activity"; or "that's really interesting, tell me more about it." Specific kinds of descriptive questions include

(1) grand-tour questions—a request for an overview of some matter of interest;
(2) mini-tour questions—more detailed exploration of a particular matter;
(3) example questions—requests for illustrations and examples of matters of interest;
(4) experience questions—queries about people's direct experiences or what has actually happened; and
(5) native-language questions—requests for extrapolation or clarification of particular terms, concepts, phrases, and the like used by insiders.

In asking descriptive questions, it is necessary to establish good rapport with insiders (see Blau, 1964). It is unwise to pressure people and ask questions in such a way that they feel uncomfortable. It is useful to approach people by seeking their cooperation in helping you find out about something. Let them feel as if they have special knowledge and are very important to your study. It is helpful to have insiders repeat descriptions, thereby acquiring the sense that you are especially interested and want to understand them better. This also helps you get a second look at matters of interest and correct possible misunderstandings. And it enables you to check for the consistency of information provided by the person.

Similarly, it is useful to restate what people say, giving back to them what you heard. You thereby provide further indication of your interest, leading to greater rapport, and the person being questioned has the opportunity to correct, reinforce, interpret, or otherwise clarify things. "Why" questions and questions that ask people to explain what they "mean" should be avoided (Spradley, 1979, pp. 81-83). Questions of this sort tend to pressure people and convey an evaluative judgment. This may put insiders on the defensive. Unless this is your purpose, "what," "when," "where," and especially "how" questions are more likely to result in descriptive information. In explaining "how" they do something, for instance, people also tend to provide a description of why they do it, and what it means to them.

It is not always possible to avoid placing insiders on the defensive and still ask relevant questions. People sometimes take offense or feel pressured even when you are careful to avoid these situations. It sometimes is useful to place people on the defensive by pressing them, perhaps to test for accuracy and consistency of information. In some cases it simply does not matter because they already are hostile toward you. Pressure questions are risky because people are more likely to lie or refuse to talk further in this situation, resulting in poor information or the end of the interview.

In observing and conversing with people, you most likely will encounter descriptive terms—expressed in ordinary language or jargon—for people, places, events, activities, and the like that you suspect are composed of multiple meanings, parts, or layers. In order to get a picture of what this involves, you need to ask what is included or what parts make up a particular item. An important line of questioning pertains to seeking the parts, components, aspects, phases, levels, and the like of matters discussed by insiders. My (1979) effort to understand references to an "esoteric community," as noted above, involved asking many questions about what this phenomenon included, thereby unraveling its multiple meanings and layers.

Questions seeking to *compare* and *contrast* represent still another line of inquiry. Put simply, comparison questions ask people to tell how things are like one another while contrast questions ask people to tell how things differ from one another. Questions asking for comparisons and contrasts greatly facilitate understanding what objects belong or do not belong to particular classes, as well as providing the means for distinguishing how they are or are not related to one another.

Informal Interviews

Informal interviews are like casual conversations. They differ from casual conversations mainly in being characterized specifically by a question-and-answer format. During an informal interview, you are questioning insiders about matters of interest. Like an ordinary conversation, this questioning is casual, free flowing, and unencumbered by extensive preconceptions of what and how the topics will be discussed. You may have a general set of issues to be discussed but, unlike more formal interviews, it is not necessary to ask the same questions exactly the same way each time. To move from casual questioning and interviewing to more formal interviewing strategies requires that considerable rapport with insiders has been established and that people are willing to devote time and attention to your questions. Unlike casual questioning, an informal interview may involve visible efforts on your part to record by paper and pencil or audio-tape the conversation.

By way of informal interviews, you will be able to gather information systematically. You frequently will have a general idea about a matter of interest and desire to be more certain of the insiders' perspective. By raising the same set of issues with different respondents, you are able systematically to collect information about these issues. Informal interviewing is an especially useful strategy for discerning different viewpoints held by insiders.

Formal Interviews

Formal interviews differ from informal interviews in that they employ a structured schedule of questions. Through use of this uniform schedule, you are able to ask specific questions in exactly the same way time after time with different insiders. Formal interviews, consequently, very systematically produce a highly uniform set of data. This form of interview requires that you have a definite sense of precisely what questions are relevant. It also presumes that you have established sufficient rapport with people to be able to request formal interviews with them. For these reasons, formal interviewing is most appropriate during the later stages of fieldwork. In some instances, formal interviewing is useful for quickly and efficiently collecting a uniform set of data about people who are related but not central to your investigation.

Formal interviews were conducted with all tarot card readers in the area who would agree to an interview during my participant observational study of occultism (see Jorgensen, 1979; Jorgensen and Jorgensen, 1982). Given that the occult tarot and tarot card readers had become a focal point for my inquiry, I wanted to gather a uniform set of information about them, their use of the tarot, and their views regarding its divinatory practice. I also employed a formal interview method to obtain a uniform set of data on particular groups within the community. While I had been systematically keeping records about particular groups encountered in the field, a sizable proportion of the groups on my list had not been investigated formally. I, therefore, interviewed a representative from as many groups as could be contacted by telephone. This procedure is not especially useful for gathering in-depth information. It was extremely useful, however, for collecting uniform data about characteristic beliefs, practices employed by the group, relationships with other groups, estimates of the number of members, and general characteristics of members (age, gender, and so on).

Formal interviews very much resemble structured questionnaires. These instruments consist of a standard set of questions. The answers to questions may be formulated in an *open-ended* fashion, thereby permitting insiders to provide their own meanings. Typically, however, respondents are required to make a *forced choice* among a *fixed* number of responses defined in advance by the researcher. An interview schedule is administered by a researcher in a face-to-face situation or some approximation of it, such as by telephone. A questionnaire is a self-administered device that can be completed by respondents without the assistance of or face-to-face contact with the researcher. Questionnaires, consequently, enable the researcher to collect information without having actually to be present. The instrument may be left and picked up or returned later. It may be distributed by the researcher, research assistants, people willing to help, or even sent through the mail.

The advantages of formal interviews and questionnaires include the collection of a highly uniform set of information, the possibility of reaching more people with less investment of the researcher's time (as compared to participant observation), and the use of more quantitative measurement techniques. In comparison with other forms of data collected during participant observation, formal interviews and questionnaires generally result in less richly qualitative information. The resulting information generally is more superficial, more difficult to interpret, and subject to suspicions difficult to explore by these methods (Douglas, 1985). At best, formal interviews and questionnaires are a supplementary means of gathering data during participant observation. Within these limitations, formal interviews and questionnaires can be an effective way of gathering information. Because of the researcher's participant familiarity with the problem, some of the troubles associated with use of these techniques alone—the relevancy of questions and answers for insiders, truthfulness of responses, honesty of respondents, and so on—are minimized.

Fine (1987) supplemented participant observation by using a questionnaire to collect data on Little League baseball. Peshkin (1986) employed assistants to gather a uniform set of data systematically from students at a fundamentalist Christian school, thereby supplementing participant observation. Fischer (1979) used informal and formal interviews with teenagers during a participant observational study of adolescent pregnancy.

In-Depth Interviews and Life Histories

A very special form of interviewing commonly associated with participant observation is the in-depth interview or in-depth probe (see Douglas, 1976, 1985). In-depth interviews depend heavily on informal interviewing techniques, but they also may include more formal interviews and even questionnaires. In-depth interviews differ from other strategies in that they seek to explore particular matters in elaborate and comprehensive detail. To accomplish this, the in-depth interview may run two hours, three hours, or even more, and it may take place over a rather extended time period. The same person, in other words, may be interviewed on different occasions for several hours over days, weeks, or even months.

In-depth interviews are especially valuable when participant observation has resulted in the identification of particular people who are especially knowledgeable about a matter of interest. "Informants," as these types of people sometimes are called, have extensive knowledge and they may be willing to talk or be interviewed intensively. During the study of occultism, my tarot teacher, for instance, was such a person. He had been involved in occultism for over thirty years. He knew the local scene intimately, and he had participated in similar scenes in other parts of the country. On the basis of our close friendship, he was willing to talk with me at great length. Many of our conversations ran three and four hours, and I was free to call him almost anytime to seek information or clarification of particular points of interest.

Not uncommonly, key informants also turn out to be competent native observers. Once they understand what you are after, they are able and willing to assist in data collection. Sometimes researchers cultivate these relationships explicitly in order to turn these people into field assistants. Hughes (1977) depended on former addicts as participant observers for the collection of descriptive information about this scene. Similarly, Zimmerman and Weider (1977) employed students as informers and field-workers to investigate drug subcultures.

The in-depth interview may lead to an interest in the entire life of an insider or insiders. When this happens, the product takes the form of a life history (see Bertaux, 1981). This method was pioneered by Thomas and Znaniecki (1918-19), who collected the biography of a Polish American peasant to investigate immigrant adjustments to urban life and the larger processes of social change. Life histories have been used profitably for studies of crime and criminal careers. Sutherland studied the professional thief through in-depth interviews and life history methods (see Sutherland and Conwell, 1967). Klockars (1974) used participant observation and interviewing methods to collect the life history of a professional fence. Dollard (1937) gathered extensive life histories of "Negroes" during a participant observational study of "caste and class in a southern town."

DOCUMENTS AND HUMAN ARTIFACTS

In the course of participant observation, most researchers encounter a wide array of human communications, especially documents of many different varieties, as well as other human artifacts ranging from tools, machines, and clothing to handicrafts and art. These products of human activity potentially provide rich sources of secondary, and in some cases even primary, research materials. In most cases, data of this sort represent naturally occurring phenomena ripe with human meanings.

Manning (1977, 1980) made extensive use of many forms of communication (movies, television, newspapers, magazines) in participant observational studies of police. Johnson (1975) supplemented participant observation of welfare workers with reviews of organizational records and case files. Bromley and Shupe (1979) depended heavily on many different forms of documents produced by marginal religious groups and their opponents during their participant observational studies (see also, Shupe and Bromley, 1980).

In the esoteric community I (see Jorgensen, 1979) studied, there were many different sources of documents. American occultism rests on a huge volume of literature representing Western cultural traditions extending back at least to the Renaissance. I read widely in this literature, focusing on the social history of the occult tarot to guide selection of materials. This literature served to provide a general background on specific occultisms, like the tarot, and its divinatory practice, and it generally prepared me to understand better the insiders' world of meaning and action.

Three organizations provided a steady stream of writings directly pertinent to the local scene. These invaluable documents included codes of ethics and conduct; lists of related groups and individuals defining the community and particular networks and segments; articles devoted to outlining correct beliefs and specific practices; editorials concerned with political aspects of the community and its relationship to the larger society; and biographical information about well-known local leaders and occult practitioners. These materials were extremely useful in providing unobtrusive support for and illustrations of findings derived from participant observation and interviewing.

Documents, in many cases, are not restricted to written materials. Within the esoteric community, I collected audiotape recordings of divinatory readings, instructions about belief and practice, and the like. Some occultists maintained video recordings of occult practices as well as slides and photographs of matters of interest. Like written materials, this information greatly enhanced and enriched findings derived from participant observation.

Aside from collecting written documents of all varieties, I began a collection of tarot card decks, most of which were readily available from local specialty shops or particular groups. Had they been of interest in terms of the problem I was studying, many other artifacts such as jewelry, paintings and other artwork, and tools of the trade (crystals, including crystal balls that mediums use for occult divination) also were collectible in this setting. Artifacts such as these sometimes serve as a distinctive basis for inquiry in and of themselves, not just as a source of support for other findings.

Altheide (1976) has made extensive use of videotapes and newspapers in participant observational investigations of news making. Documents in this case greatly enhance data collected by way of direct observation and interviewing. Conversely, Altheide (1987) argues, participant observation improves comprehension and analysis of documents.

PERSONAL EXPERIENCE

Personal experience derived from direct participation in the insiders' world is an extremely valuable source of information, especially if the researcher has performed membership roles and otherwise experienced life as an insider (see Adler and Adler, 1987). By becoming a member, the researcher generates the experiences of a member. As a researcher, you should be properly critical of personal experience—just like any other information. Yet your experiences—because they are your experiences—are subject to even more critical examination than the experiences of other members.

During the study of occultists (see Jorgensen, 1979), my performance of the seeker, client, and reader roles provided direct experience of the insiders' world from different membership standpoints. Description of the occult community was enhanced greatly by these personal experiences. Performance of the tarot card reader role proved especially valuable as a source of information. Prior to full assumption of this role, I had a vague notion of the culture of occult practitioners. I had, for instance, been able to identify a formal code of ethics, informal guidelines for practice, and technical procedures for performing divination. As an insider, however, this information came to take on new meanings. I learned of readers' conceptions of clientele, informal norms of practice, and many of the means whereby more formal social structures are translated into day-to-day activities.

The contentions of outsiders that occultists engage in con artistry and fraud acquired new meaning (see Jorgensen, 1984). I discovered from personal experience that readers recognize and carefully manage self-presentations in such a way as to create and sustain the impression for believers that something extraordinary is happening. Yet they are disdainful of explicitly fraudulent practices. They shun techniques referred to as "cold reading" that some people use to dupe clients. Given that the very theory and structure of most divinatory techniques— whatever their ultimate ontological status—provide means to achieve a sincerely felt sense of having accomplished divination, most of these people simply have little use for con artistry. If nothing else, con artistry was a performance more difficult to manage than simply employing readily available means for predicting past, present, and future events.

Personal experience, therefore, was invaluable in several ways. By doing something myself, I was able actually to *feel* it from the standpoint of an insider. Emotions and feelings otherwise are extremely difficult to investigate. Personal experience thereby is a principal way of gaining access to this absolutely crucial aspect of human existence. On this basis, it is possible to generate new understandings of particular ways of life. I was able, for instance, to use personal experience as a source of new questions to be checked out by further questioning of insiders. And personal experience provided a way in which theretofore impersonal and abstract meanings could be verified. It was very important that, by verifying information through my own experience, I was able to gain a profound sense of particular subtleties of the way of life I was studying.

SUMMARY

The methodology of participant observation depends on observation as a basic strategy for gathering facts. Direct experience and observation is the mainstay of this methodology. Participant observers employ interview strategies, ranging from highly informal, casual conversations to formal interviews and questionnaires. The participant observer usually has access to a wide range of human communications and artifacts. Human communications, especially in the form of documents, include letters, diaries, memoranda, written records of all sorts, promotional literature, books, magazine articles, and journals. In most human settings, it is possible to gather other artifacts, such as clothing, pictures, artwork, and tools. Observation and other strategies of data collection are part of the larger process of inquiry that participant observers use to focus and refine issues of study.

EXERCISES

1. Select a setting for observation (schools, churches, public parks, bars, courtrooms, banks, families, clubs, and the like generally are readily

available settings). Spend an hour or so observing this setting, keeping a record (notes) of your observations. Discuss your observation in terms of what you observed, why you focused on this rather than something else, what you selected to note, and so on. Did you have trouble observing? Discuss any difficulties you experienced.

2. Identify a topic of interest and several relevant people to interview. Conduct an informal interview with at least one person. Use this information to construct a short interview schedule and formally interview one more person. Compare and contrast the information collected by the informal and formal interview strategies. What are the strengths and weaknesses of these methods?

3. Select an example of participant observation from the literature. To what extent did the researcher use direct observation, interviewing, personal experience, documents, or other methods? What kinds of information were collected through these different strategies? Briefly discuss the advantages and disadvantages of these methods of data collection.

4. Personal experience, it has been argued here, is an invaluable source of information. List, from your own experience and history, some of the ways that personal experience has been useful to your education. Is personal experience more or less trustworthy than other forms of information? Why or why not?

7

Notes, Records, and Files

This chapter presents principles and strategies for creating, developing, and maintaining notes, records, and files. Technologies appropriate for making notes and records are reviewed. A variety of basic types and forms of notes, records, and files are discussed and illustrated.

NOTES AND RECORDS

Making notes, keeping records, and creating data files are among the most important aspects of participant observation. As you become immersed in a setting, there is a temptation to concentrate on observation and participation, postponing and neglecting to make notes and records. This is a mistake. The human memory, even one expanded and disciplined by practice in the field, is undependable. The longer you wait to record observations, the more will be lost from conscious awareness, sometimes forever. The value of getting into a routine of regularly making notes and records during or shortly after periods of direct involvement in the field cannot be overemphasized.

The type, form, and content of the notes you create depend on personal preference and style, the issues studied, the setting and situations of observation, and the technologies used. You should record dates, times, places; the statuses, roles, and activities of key people; and major activities and events. Casual conversations and interviews should be recorded. You will find it useful to make notes regarding personal feelings, hunches, guesses, and speculations. Notes and files may be handwritten; typewritten; recorded by still photography, audio-video equipment, and audiotape; or processed on a computer. Once created, records require organization and analysis.

Ideally, your notes would provide a literal record of everything transpiring in the field setting. Obviously, this is very unrealistic. You may have difficulty, especially during the early stages of fieldwork, even deciding what is noteworthy. Where, then, do you begin?

Mundane Facts

An excellent place to begin your preliminary note making is with the mundane facts of a setting, those routine features that otherwise go unnoticed and are largely taken for granted. By describing the physical surroundings, the characteristics of people and their activities, for instance, you become conscious of even the most obvious features of the setting, and you can experiment with and practice making notes and records. While in the field, it is very useful to keep a running record, or chronology, of the highlights of participation and observation. Make at least a brief record of what happened, why, involving whom, where, and any analytic comments you may have about these matters. Even if you fail to provide detailed accounts of events, these notes will enable you to recall issues of possible importance later.

For instance, you might begin by describing the physical environment. What is the physical location? If it is a building, what is its layout and how is this space used by people? Likewise, you might describe the general social environment. How many people are there? What are the social characteristics of these people? Are you able to discern or collect information about people's age, gender, ethnicity, socioeconomic status, education, occupation, and so on? How are people arranged in this environment? What are people doing? How are people related? How are their activities organized? Is there a sequence or a pattern to events? What are their beliefs? It is perhaps obvious that particular field settings will suggest many other specific issues of possible interest.

Hayano's (1982) early field notes from participant observation with poker players, for instance, were jotted down occasionally and somewhat haphazardly. He frequently traveled for several hours getting to and from poker playing situations. Eventually he decided to use this time for tape-recording field notes more regularly, comprehensively, and systematically. Altheide (1976) similarly used a tape recorder to note observations of television news making. After a day of participant observation, he would think aloud about what had happened, debriefing himself, and highlighting whatever seemed important at the time. I (see Jorgensen, 1979) usually spent several hours in the evening after a day's participant observation of occultists typewriting field notes. Like Hayano, my early note making was irregular and unsystematic. In making notes, I mixed descriptions of field observations and experiences with lengthy effort at analysis, constantly seeking to refine and focus the issues to be studied. Though rather crude, my notes resembled a report of findings, because they included much discussion of theory and data.

Central Topics and Problems

After a brief period of fieldwork, you most likely will begin to develop
a priority of interests. Questions will begin to emerge and guide
subsequent participation and observation. While these matters may
change constantly as you seek to refine and focus the problem of study,
at any given time you should be able to identify particular topics or
problems of special interest. Your note making efforts should concentrate on these matters, whatever they are.

At least until you have a more certain idea about the precise focus and
problem to be studied, your note keeping should aim to be as literal and
comprehensive as you have time, ability, and energy to manage. Do not
be afraid to be flexible and imaginative in your note taking. In some
cases you may find it useful to begin with a simple idea or matter of
interest and see where it takes you. Matters that do not seem especially
important at one point in time frequently become important or lead to
the collection of important data later.

Making notes is not only important, it is exceptionally time consuming. For every hour of fieldwork, you may spend two, three, or more
hours describing and analyzing what you experienced and observed,
especially if you make written notes. Although you should not neglect
fieldwork, note making and observation very much are interrelated.
Making records of what you observed helps clarify and organize your
thinking. It commonly leads to the identification of matters of importance
for subsequent observation that have been overlooked or neglected.
Conducting fieldwork based on these insights, in turn, will provide new
material for notes and records, analysis, and subsequent observation.

As the issues and problem of investigation become more concisely
defined, your notes should concentrate more systematically on describing
these interests in considerable detail. You will need to have fairly accurate
and detailed records of daily observations, casual conversations, informal
interviews, and especially more formal interviews. Like all field notes,
these observations should be tied closely to the reality, especially the
language, of the people with whom you are interacting. Whenever
possible, conversations with insiders should aim to provide a literal, even
verbatim, record. I used a tape recorder, for instance, to create a verbatim
record of tarot card readings. These recordings were the basis for
subsequent analysis of occult divination (see Jorgensen, 1984).

In some instances, you will be forced to depend on your memory.
With practice, you should become increasingly expert in recalling

literally the sequence of events, phrases of conversation, and even actual jargon employed by people. Recall is better within a few minutes and hours of fieldwork than over longer periods of time. Sometimes it is useful to make a few notes and then do something else (like sleep) before writing up these notes. This strategy may be especially useful if you are deeply immersed in the setting, because even a short distance from events tends to bring them into clear perspective. Do not wait too long, however, as after more than a day or two you will forget the details of most observational experiences. In recalling field experiences, it may be useful to transport yourself mentally back into the situation and imaginatively reconstruct events as you make notes.

Telling someone about what happened serves the same purpose. It is very helpful to have a friend, associate, companion, spouse, colleague, or adviser who is willing to debrief you regularly. Discussion with interested parties is especially useful if they will ask questions and raise issues for discussion. In this way, you may uncover neglected matters or unseen issues, gain a new appreciation for what has become routine to you, or simply have an opportunity to explore hunches and suspicions. The Adlers, for instance, spent many hours talking over their participant observation of drug dealing and analyzing these data by talks with their adviser, Douglas (see Adler, 1985; Adler and Adler, 1987). I spent five or more hours a week debriefing Rambo (1987) during her participant observation of exotic dancers.

After extensive participant observation with professional card-players, Hayano (1982) began to focus attention on observing and recording particular features of the field setting. He began to see such issues as how poker players selected card rooms and games, how they defined other players, playing strategies, norms of playing, and notions of luck and misfortune as central activities and issues of study. His notes consequently aimed to describe these categories of activity and the activities themselves in the ordinary language terms of insiders. In other words, Hayano carefully listened to insiders and recorded in their own words what aspects of poker playing were and were not most important, and the meanings players assigned to their activities. Public table talk was extensive in this setting and served as the fundamental basis for Hayano's observations and records. He, therefore, engaged in little formal interviewing of people.

Preble and Casey (1969) had been involved in the participant observational study of heroin addicts for a lengthy period of time when Preble and Miller (1977) set out to study the effect of large-scale methadone maintenance treatment programs on the lives of addicts. They consequently were fairly certain of the basic problem and issues to be studied. Aside from being interested in the subculture of urban addicts, Preble and Miller used participant observation to collect demographic data: they counted the number of drug users in the area studied block by block and recorded the age, gender, ethnicity, and habit of addicts. Because they were interested at the outset in gathering this specific information, their record keeping, likewise, reflected a high degree of certainty. While recording specific information derived from participant observation and various forms of interviewing (casual conversations, formal interviews with key informants, life histories), this team remained open to the discovery of new patterns of street life. When you have certain information to collect, it may be possible to construct a schedule for recording this information, while using more free-form notes to record emergent findings that were unanticipated.

Feelings, Hunches, and Impressions

Participant observers find it extremely useful to note and record their personal feelings and impressions of field involvements and data collection. If only for therapeutic reasons, it is useful to note your fears, apprehensions, mistakes, and misadventures as well as your excitements, successes, and major accomplishments. It is also valuable to note guesses, hunches, suspicions, predictions, and areas of neglect as well as topics in need of subsequent inquiry. Notes about these matters tend to be extremely useful in judging the course of your inquiry, developing future courses of action in the field, and as part of making preliminary sense out of the materials you have been collecting (see Johnson, 1975; Glazer and Strauss, 1967).

RECORDING TECHNOLOGIES

Participant observational notes may be recorded by way of a variety of technologies. Field-workers find pencil and paper useful to some extent. Machine technologies, such as the typewriter and, increasingly, word processors, however, have become the mainstay of field notes and records. Audio recordings are invaluable as either a method of recording actual field conversations and events or as a means of keeping notes. Still photography is an excellent way of preserving realistic images of people, objects, and places. Audio-video technologies enable researchers to capture both verbal and visual events in a permanent record.

Pencil and Paper

Pencil-and-paper notes are useful when you need to record something briefly. In most field situations, it is possible to jot something down quickly without being too obtrusive. You usually can make pencil-and-paper notes under conditions where it would be impossible to use a portable personal computer or even an audiotape recorder.

Though indispensable, the uses of pencil-and-paper notes are seriously limited (see Whyte, 1955). Handwritten notes are bulky and more difficult to read than notes printed on a machine. It is extremely difficult, even if you employ shorthand, to make a verbatim record in this way. It is difficult to analyze materials in this form. Handwritten notes frequently must be transformed before attempting serious analysis. This not uncommonly means spending hours typing or word processing them.

Use handwritten, paper-and-pencil notes in those situations where some kind of a record is needed and it is not possible or reasonable to use any other technology. An audiotape recorder is much better for making a literal record of conversation. Tape-recorded notes also are more efficient to make. People talk faster and more accurately than they write. Handwritten or tape-recorded notes will have to be word processed, however, in order to be analyzed efficiently. When possible, you should consider using a word processor in the first place, thereby saving considerable time.

Audio Recordings

Audio recordings are excellent for making notes. Recorders are readily available, relatively inexpensive, and easy to operate. Standard cassette recorders about the size of an ordinary paperback book work nicely, especially in the field. For highly covert fieldwork, there are smaller, mini-cassette recorders. There is no better way at the present time to record verbal interaction, especially interviews, than audiocassette recorders.

Tape recorders are obtrusive. Altheide (1976) reports abandoning use of the recorder for casual conversations and interviews with television newspeople because of their tendency to perform for the recorder. In some settings, the presence of a tape recorder may be normalized. People commonly forget the recorder is running after a brief period, or come to take it for granted. I was able to tape-record divinatory readings of the tarot as a normal part of interaction without any mention of research. Therapy sessions, organizational meetings, lectures, and the like commonly are tape-recorded.

In many fieldwork situations, it is possible to use tape recorders as an alternative to paper-and-pencil notes. You may be able to record notes while participating, during breaks in the action, or shortly after periods of field involvement. During a participant observational study of social welfare organizations, Johnson (1975), for instance, made use of audio recorders in all of these ways.

In spite of the advantages of recorders for making notes, ultimately the tapes require transcription, whether for analysis or illustration. This is time consuming and it is expensive if someone else has to be hired. You should consider this disadvantage in deciding whether or not to use a tape recorder. You most likely will find recorders useful for certain purposes even if you decide to limit the volume of notes made with this technology.

Computers

A typewriter may be used to construct field notes, but this technology has been rendered obsolete by computers. With a computer and word processor, you will be able to create field notes, arrange them in files, and manipulate these files analytically. Almost any computer is useful. Highly portable computers greatly facilitate movement in the field setting (see Kirk, 1981). If you do not already use a computer, you should be able to learn enough in a few hours to begin creating notes. It frequently is possible to link computers together, connecting home and office, coworkers, colleagues, or students and instructors. To create field notes, word processing software is required for the computer (see Conrad and Reinhartz, 1984). The word processor will enable you to create notes by keying in the data arranged as files. Once entered, you will be able to copy material, rearrange it, and otherwise manipulate it for particular analytic purposes.

Photography

Still photography is an outstanding way to note observations when a literal visual record is necessary or desirable (see Bateson and Mead, 1942;

Collier, 1967; Hocking, 1975; Bellman and Jules-Rosette, 1977; Becker, 1981). Photographic records rarely are sufficient in and of themselves, but fieldwork may be conducted more efficiently and with enhanced quality through photography. Photographs efficiently capture visual aspects of field locations and settings. Several hours' verbal description of the setting may be reduced to a few minutes of photography. These records sometimes preserve important, though not readily apparent, details for subsequent analysis. Like tape recorders, however, cameras may be highly obtrusive or routine depending on the setting.

The camera is an extension of visual perception. Photographs reflect the culture of the user. People decide what to photograph, how it is framed and focused, and so on. Although a photograph reflects the sociocultural outlook of the operator, it is a useful tool: It mechanically records; it does not fatigue; and it permits comparison, sorting, analysis, and interpretation, in much the same way as verbal or written records. While it may not be a primary source of recording notes, it frequently is an indispensable supplementary method of making notes and records. Aside from being a way of recording the visual details of the physical environment, photography is especially useful for making records of *nonverbal* human scenes and interactions (see Bateson and Mead, 1942; Hall, 1959, 1966, 1976; Birdwhistell, 1952; Vesperi, 1985). Photography sometimes is an excellent way of initiating rapport with the natives. People, in other words, oftentimes like to have their pictures taken. Start by photographing public scenes before using the camera in more private settings.

Audio-Video Equipment

It has become practical in recent years to use audio-video equipment (film or preferably videotape) to make records of participant observation. Unlike still photography, this technology records movement and action. The use of audio-video tape recording equipment in participant observational research shares all of the disadvantages of audiotape recording and still photography. It is highly obtrusive in most situations. Audio-video records are especially useful for microscopic analyses of human interaction.

During the normal course of human interaction, it is difficult, even when there are multiple observers, to record accurately the movements and actions of people in multiparty scenes. Video equipment produces a fairly accurate and detailed record. This record may be analyzed repeatedly if necessary. Like still photography, moving picture records are subject to the perspective of the user. This technology has been used very effectively for recording religious rituals (Jules-Rosette, 1975) and interaction among schoolchildren (Mehan, 1974), among other possibilities (see Bellman and Jules-Rosette, 1977).

RECORDS AND FILES

There are many different forms appropriate for participant observational notes. Field notes and records may take the form of a running calendar of events, a daily logbook of happenings, a personal diary, a journal of fieldwork results, or preliminary drafts of findings. The participant observer may employ a very simple technology alone or use a variety of technologies, mixing means of creating notes, forms of records, and strategies for preparing materials for analysis. Try as many different strategies as seem appropriate to the problem and the setting, and experiment with new combinations or forms to see what works for you.

You need some form regularly to record daily activities. A *calendar* of events is useful for this purpose. This may be an appointment book or calendar used regularly to jot down short records. Some participant observers prefer to make more substantive notes in the form of a *logbook*. Like the calendar, the logbook is a running, chronological record of fieldwork. Unlike the calendar, it is a more substantive record of field observations and experiences.

Participant observers traditionally maintain a *field journal*. The journal commonly is a combination of calendar or appointment book and logbook, and it may include results of interviews as well as notes about personal feelings and hunches. In other words, the field journal is a reasonably comprehensive record of experiences and observations in the field.

Though rarely discussed, some participant observers developed field notes as drafts of findings addressed to a research problem. *Drafts* differ considerably from ordinary notes in that the data are treated as an integral part of emergent analytic schemes. While field notes generally are organized by times, days, settings, and particular observations or experiences, drafts are organized around theoretical issues.

Most participant observers probably do begin to write up findings before actual fieldwork is complete, whether or not they regard these drafts as a way of making notes, creating and manipulating records, conducting preliminary analyses and interpretation, and/or communicating findings. This procedure is desirable because it helps reveal gaps in the data and leads to isolating areas in need of further investigation. Preliminary drafts are not in and of themselves, however, an adequate substitute for regular, systematic records of fieldwork.

Eventually, notes and records of whatever variety must be converted to a medium appropriate for analysis and interpretation. In the past, participant observers spent many hours and even days creating files, many of them containing duplicate pieces of information, for analytic purposes (see Whyte, 1955). As field notes accumulate, they should be sorted, sifted, and arranged with an eye toward refining and focusing issues and problems of study. The tedious job of labeling, organizing, maintaining, and manipulating files containing field notes and records is efficiently conducted by computer. Word processors make it possible to create multiple copies of a set of notes, and manipulate these materials in many ways with little more investment in time and energy than it takes to input this information. Analysis and theorizing, however, are the subject of the next chapter.

SUMMARY

This chapter discussed strategies and technologies for creating notes, records, and files. You need a way or ways of briefly and regularly making note of field activities, as well as procedures for more systematically and comprehensively recording observations, personal experiences, casual conversations, interviews, and anything else of possible importance that occurs during fieldwork. Constructing notes and records is an integral part of the methodology of participant observation. Through record keeping, your thinking is clarified and you are able to work different perspectives on emergent findings, thereby reformulating plans for subsequent data collection. In creating notes, you may find it useful to employ paper and pencil, audio recorders, cameras, or computers. Computer word processors are especially useful for organizing and manipulating field notes and files.

EXERCISES

1. Select some setting for observation, preferably one with lots of action. Enlist the cooperation of a friend or classmate to observe and make notes

about this setting. (This works best with two or more people, but one person may play both roles.) One of you observe only, and the other one of you observe and make notes of what transpires. After two or three days, have the person who simply observed write up what he or she observed. Compare and contrast these two methods. In what ways are they different? Is one set of notes better or worse than the other? If so, in what ways is one set of notes better than the other?

2. Select a setting of observation (a school, bank, park, bar, courtroom, or the like), participate and observe briefly, making notes. Try several different methods of recording observations, such as paper-and-pencil notes, audio recordings, and still photography. Compare and contrast these procedures for making notes, and discuss the relative merits of them.

3. Try keeping a running account, logbook, or journal of your everyday life experiences (or focus specifically on a particular aspect of your existence such as school, family, or job). Describe and discuss how you did this, paying special attention to difficulties you encountered. What did you do to overcome problems? How is this exercise relevant to participant observation?

4. Select an article or book exemplifying participant observation. Review the means used to construct notes and files. Were these methods effective? Why or why not? What, if anything, would you do differently?

8

Analyzing and Theorizing

This chapter discusses and illustrates principles and procedures for analyzing and theorizing from the standpoint of the methodology of participant observation. Strategies for coding, filing, disassembling, arranging, organizing, and otherwise making sense of information collected in the field are presented. Different conceptions of theory and theorizing are reviewed and discussed critically.

THE ANALYTIC CYCLE

Analysis is a breaking up, separating, or disassembling of research materials into pieces, parts, elements, or units. With facts broken down into manageable pieces, the researcher sorts and sifts them, searching for types, classes, sequences, processes, patterns, or wholes. The aim of this process is to assemble or reconstruct the data in meaningful or comprehensible fashion. In making sense of the data, you are engaged in theorizing—the construction of meaningful patterns and organizations of facts. A theory is an arrangement of facts in the form of an explanation or interpretation.

From the standpoint of the methodology of participant observation, analyzing and theorizing are part of a larger process of inquiry. The collection of information, particularly in the form of notes and files, is sufficient to initiate the cycle of analysis. During the early stages of inquiry, you generally concentrate on gaining entrée, developing and sustaining field relations, participating, observing, and gathering information while engaging tentatively in analysis and theorizing. Analysis at this point is focused on uncovering specific issues of study and/or refining the research problem. As the issues and problem of study become more clearly defined, data collection becomes the primary activity. As you amass materials and analyze them, the collection of additional information generally becomes less important, giving way to a growing need to concentrate on the analysis of these materials.

CODING AND FILING

The analysis of data collected in the field is greatly facilitated by having this information in the form of notes that may be arranged and rearranged, coded, and collected in files. Notes should be reviewed on a regular basis, identified and labeled whenever possible as being related in particular ways to the emergent issues of study. Your reasons for collecting the information and making notes provide a basis for identifying and labeling these materials as a member of some class, type, or set, as part of or related to a sequence, process, or pattern. In other words, you need to specify how a fact or set of facts is related to the issues you are studying. Facts do not speak for themselves! They do not make sense except by reference to some intellectual context or framework you employ to render them sensible and meaningful. The range of possible meanings ultimately is limited; however, there usually are several possible readings of the data. You may need to establish the grounds for deciding among different possible interpretations of the data. In spite of tremendous differences among research topics, problems, frames of reference, and so on, it is possible to raise a set of questions useful for coding and labeling your field notes.

One analytic strategy is to identify and label a phenomenon in terms of its basic components. In doing this, you may be able to identify what parts are more and less essential to the phenomenon. Can you, for instance, identify certain features, pieces, components, or elements making up a phenomenon. Is it possible to identify and label constituent elements? Are some of these parts more or less important or essential? If you remove a particular element (perhaps only imaginatively) of some phenomenon, does it change or remain the same? If it changes, what does this involve? For instance, take a belief or ideology (such as "women are superior to men," "delinquency results from bad homes," "Americans are superior to other people") and see if you can identify its basic components by references to some body of data (what some collection of people say and do). Damrell (1977) extensively employs the analytic strategy of examining phenomena for their essential features in a participant observational study of seeking spiritual meaning through Hindu (Vedanta) religion.

Looking for patterns and relationships among facts is another analytic strategy. Put simply, do the facts you are analyzing constitute or form some discernible pattern? What, if any, are the connections or relationships among particular pieces of information? It frequently is useful to ask whether or not the matter in question is part of some larger sequence of events or process, and where it does or does not fit into this larger scheme.

Spradley (1970), for instance, found that tramps (urban alcoholics) experience getting put in jail (called making the bucket) as a ritual, a sequence composed of distinctive stages. Making the bucket involves (1) the street (pinch); (2) call box (shake down by cops); (3) paddy wagon (pick up); (4) elevator (work over by cops); (5) booking desk (shake down); (6) padded drunk tank (throw in); (7) x-ray, mug, and print room (work over); (8) cement drunk tank (stall); (9) court docket (call name); (10) courtroom (give time); (11) holding tank (make a lockup); (12) delousing tank (sit bare ass); (13-a) trusty tank (bust); (13-b) time tank (lock up); and (14) booking desk (make a kickout).

Comparing and contrasting is another valuable analytic strategy. Is the fact in question the same as or similar to other phenomena? Is it different from other facts? Identifying similarities and differences among phenomena generally enables you to arrange facts into classes, types, or sets. On this basis, you will be able to apply an emergent typology to analyze further additional phenomena. It also is useful to inquire whether or not the types you have identified are related to other forms. In other words, are there linkages or relationships among or between classes of facts?

Manning (1980), for example, found two contrasting types of organizational control of drug investigations among police assigned to narcotics. An *organization*-centered type of control may be distinguished from an *investigator*-centered type of control. Each of these forms of controlling drug investigations is identified by a set of contrasting characteristics, such as whether or not a written record is required, whether or not cases are officially opened or closed, whether or not it is possible to calculate clearance rates, the use of informants, and whose approval or supervision is required.

It is helpful when engaging in analysis to ask different questions and to phrase these questions in different ways. For instance, ask a question in a positive fashion and then turn it around and ask it negatively. Spradley might have asked, for instance, how many ways are there of making a bucket? Or he might have questioned: Which of these materials I have been examining are not part of or related to making a bucket? It sometimes is useful, furthermore, to try a different order of question, or a different logic. To illustrate, Manning might have asked: How are drug investigations accomplished organizationally? What are the steps of a drug investigation? Or perhaps, In what ways do narcotics investigations differ from one another?

Initial efforts to code and label notes commonly involve a single word or phrase used to mark pieces of field data. As your problem of study is refined and focused, a general schema for coding frequently emerges, and you become more proficient at its use. The codes or key words used, in other words, will become more precisely defined, you will begin to develop connections among them, and you will develop greater facility in applying the labels to research materials. Efforts to code field notes eventually will result in more lengthy discussions of relevant issues as you review and work with these materials.

SORTING, SIFTING, CONSTRUCTING, AND RECONSTRUCTING

Efforts to code data will lead to sorting, sifting, organizing, and reorganizing these materials, usually into larger units and components. Sometimes this involves flashes of insight about how things fit together, while at other times it depends on less dramatic hunches, or simply hard work. Is a pattern or type discernible? Is some sequence or process apparent? Can you ascertain connections or relationships among concepts? Is some sequence or process apparent? Can you ascertain connections or relationships among concepts?

As different ways of arranging materials are explored, you may find it useful to consult or revisit existing literature and theories related to your problem. Hayano (1982), for instance, was thoroughly immersed in the world of professional gamblers and deeply involved in observing and describing the insiders' world of meaning and experience when he began comparing his data with existing literature and theorizing. In working with data on occultists, I (1979) found it necessary to revisit literature as different issues emerged from analysis. While it is important to consult existing literature, you should not be constrained by what other people have done. Use your imagination! The analysis of data leading to discovery requires creativity.

The analysis of qualitative data is dialectical: Data are disassembled into elements and components; these materials are examined for patterns and relationships, sometimes in connection to ideas derived from literature, existing theories, or hunches that have emerged during fieldwork or perhaps simply commonsense suspicions. With an idea in hand, the data are reassembled, providing an interpretation or explanation of a question or particular problem; this synthesis is then evaluated and critically examined; it may be accepted or rejected entirely or with modifications; and, not uncommonly, this process then is repeated to test further the emergent theoretical conception, expand its generality, or otherwise examine its usefulness.

Early in fieldwork on occultism, I (see Jorgensen, 1979, 1982, 1984) identified three distinctive networks of local occult practitioners and groups through an analysis of field data. Much later, in-depth interviews were conducted with tarot card readers. In analyzing the interview data, I applied the previous concept of segments of occultists in the local community. I reasoned that if this concept were correct, it would be possible to locate tarot card readers in this context. It was possible to locate tarot card readers in this scheme, but there were certain exceptions, leading me to question certain aspects of the conceptual framework. It consequently was necessary to rethink this framework and modify it based on the interview data. Hence, an emergent analytic scheme (the ideological orientations of three segments of what occultists called the "esoteric community") was used (and tested) by in-depth interview data. In turn, the interview data required that the original analytic frame be modified, clarifying the concept of the community, networks, and ideology, and how these components were connected in the everyday life existence of occultists.

THEORY AND THEORIZING

As you sort, sift, arrange, and rearrange the data and analytic labels and comments about them, it will be increasingly necessary to become more directly and explicitly involved in theory and theorizing. The methodology of participant observation involves several different forms of theory and theorizing. These forms include analytic induction, sensitizing concepts, grounded theory, existential theory, and hermeneutic (or interpretative) theory.

Analytic Induction

Znaniecki (1934, 1952, 1965) advanced a very influential conception of theory as constructed through a process of "analytic induction." He

(1935, pp. 259-60) outlined four steps to this procedure: (1) determine the essential characteristics of a given class of facts; (2) abstract these features, assuming hypothetically that the more basic are more general than the less essential, and are found in a larger variety of forms; (3) test this contention by researching classes containing the former and the latter class characteristics; and (4) organize these classes into a system based on the functions of the characteristic in determining the particular form. Put simply, analytic induction *generalizes* from the data by *abstraction*. This is very important because Znaniecki (1934, pp. 213-248) opposes forming inductive generalizations by counting the frequency of instances of some phenomena, especially through the use of statistics.

Explanations, for Znaniecki (1934, pp. 16-21), are formed through generalizations about components of a theoretical system. These explanations may be causal, functional, or genetic. Genetic explanations deal with the origins of systems or the emergence of new forms. Within a limited system, the internal order of components may be explained by the functional dependence or interdependence of elements. Causal generalizations apply to cases in which a system undergoes change that otherwise cannot be explained by its internal dynamic order. Analytic induction has been used by several generations of social scientists for constructing theories (see, for example, Angell, 1936; Lindesmith, 1947; Cressey, 1953; Bruyn, 1966).

Sensitizing Concepts

The idea of theory as "sensitizing concepts" was developed by Blumer (1954, 1969). While operational definitions and measures may result in technical precision, they tend to misconstrue the empirical world, trivialize it, and otherwise lack genuine relevance to empirical realities. Theory, Blumer (1969, p. 143) argued, "is of value in empirical science only to the extent to which it connects fruitfully with the empirical world." The aim of theory is to generate analytical schemes of the empirical world. Unlike concepts defined and measured in operational terms, *sensitizing concepts* serve to alert the user to the general character of the empirical world, by providing hints and suggestions illustrated by actual empirical cases. Theory serves as a useful and practical guide to research.

Sensitizing concepts require the user to examine carefully the uniqueness of the phenomenon under consideration and its connectedness to other phenomena within the natural environment.

Through such an examination, concepts are tested, improved, and refined. The validity of sensitizing concepts is verified through careful study of empirical cases. A participant observer, for instance, examines within the world of everyday life exactly when, where, how, and to what extent theoretical ideas do or do not apply. In this way, concepts sensitizing scholars to the realities of human existence are tested, verified, refined, or rejected *empirically*.

Grounded Theory

Glazer and Strauss (1967), like Blumer, have been concerned with linking theory and research. Their approach, called "grounded theory," depends on participant observation (see Schatzman and Strauss, 1973) and a method of comparative analysis aimed at constructing theories *inductively*. Their "constant comparative method" of analysis involves four stages: (1) comparing the data applicable to each conceptual category; (2) integrating the categories and their properties; (3) delimiting the emergent theory; and (4) writing up the theory (Glazer and Strauss, 1967, pp. 105-115).

The first step requires the analyst to code each piece of data in terms of as many analytic/conceptual categories as applicable. These categories derive from the problems or questions of study as well as ideas emergent from participant observation. The coded data also are compared with previously coded materials in the same and different categories. Comparison should lead to development of the theoretical properties of each category (the elements constituting it).

The second step involves an effort to integrate the conceptual categories and the properties of these categories. As the analyst compares pieces of data with possible conceptual categories, attention tends to shift from a focus on the evidence and categories to consideration of the properties of the categories and comparison of categories. The analyst should begin to gain some insight into how these categories are or are not related in some larger configuration.

The third step of this method is to begin actually defining and specifying the emergent theory or theoretical claims and contentions. As the analyst works through coding and comparing, and identifies the properties of concepts as well as the connections among ideas, a basic interpretative framework or theory emerges as a more or less integrated whole. The emergent theory is then tested against the data, most likely resulting in further definition or refinement of the basic conceptual categories, as well as the linkages and relationships among them. Once the analyst finds that existing categories are capable of handling most or all empirical instances pertinent to them, for instance, these categories have demonstrated their usefulness and power.

The fourth step is to write up the theory. By this point the analyst should have a body of coded data, and analytic descriptions of the concepts, properties, and relationships among them. Statement of the constructed theory involves collating, describing, and summarizing these materials as an answer to the study problem or problems (as modified throughout the research).

Existential Truth and Theory

Existential theorizing emphasizes the *existential location* of the researcher as the key to what is observed (Johnson, 1975; Douglas, 1976; Douglas and Johnson, 1977; Douglas and Rasmussen, with Flanagan, 1977; Adler, Adler, and Rochford, 1986; Kotarba and Fontana, 1984; Adler and Adler, 1987). These thinkers argue that "common sense" serves as the basis for creatively developing methods, strategies, and procedures aimed fundamentally at *practical truths* about human existence. Truths discovered through direct observation and experience are formed as *interpretative generalizations*, not absolute or formal theories. Analysis may involve many of the procedures and techniques discussed above, but it is not necessarily limited to such procedures. The existentialists have employed group debriefing and collective brainstorming sessions fruitfully as a strategy for critically reviewing and analyzing field materials.

Theory as Hermeneutics

Another view of theorizing favors disciplined *description* and *hermeneutic* (or interpretative) *understanding* (Bruyn, 1966; Geertz, 1973; Cicourel, 1974; Goffman, 1974; Agar, 1986; Clifford and Marcus, 1986). Human existence involves particular ways of life bounded by specific historical epochs. Interpretative generalizations are formed by posing questions of particular ways of life viewed as texts or wholes. In other words, the analyst addresses scholarly problems by viewing the data as representing forms of human existence to be examined by way of asking questions. The (critical) examination of the particular object of observation and inquiry may be expected to lead to some resolution and, more than likely, further questions (see Thomas, 1983).

Through a question/resolution process, a belief, practice, or entire way of life is illuminated. If further generality is desired, additional questions may be asked of the text and it may be compared with other texts. Given that the researcher and the text are historically situated, no statement of universal patterns, regularities, or laws is possible. Every generalization is an interpretation aimed at understanding, but interpretation never is absolute or complete. Interpretation is a never-ending search for understanding and enlightenment.

For example, suppose you are interested in divinatory practices. You might observe them directly or review previous studies. To construct questions, you might consider a variety of theoretical contentions, such as that people who do this are psychotic, economically or socially deprived, or seeking meaning in life. The practices themselves may be examined for problems not otherwise anticipated in existing literature. Analysis of divinatory practices might proceed by asking basic questions about the sociocultural context where these practices occur, the people who perform them, as well as the human interaction constituting divination. Resolution of such issues leads to matters of further interest, with no clear end point, except that the answer to a set of questions produced an adequate understanding, for the time being. If greater generality is necessary or desirable, you might compare and contrast divinatory practices with psychotherapy or scientific predicting. While this may satisfy (or exhaust) a certain intellectual curiosity, the ways of conceiving of divination and interpreting its significance remain unsatisfied and unexhausted in any absolute sense.

SUMMARY

This chapter described and illustrated principles and procedures for analyzing and theorizing. Analysis begins when the participant observer collects information in an everyday life setting and considers it in terms of a study problem. Analysis requires the researcher to code and label field notes—sorting, shifting, constructing, and reconstructing these materials. Analytic strategies include looking for essential features, patterns, relationships, processes, and sequences, comparing and contrasting, as well as formulating types and classes. Analysis leads directly to making sense of field data or theorizing. Theory and theorizing take a variety of forms, including analytic induction, sensitizing concepts, grounded theory, existential theory, and hermeneutic theory.

EXERCISES

1. Identify a possible question for study (such as how people make contact with one another in public settings; reasons for high school dropouts; factors leading to adolescent pregnancy; war veterans' problems readjusting to civil society) and a setting (such as a park, bar, mall, high school, vet center) for observation. Spend several hours observing and making notes. Code your notes looking for similarities, differences, essential features, classes, sequences, and so on.

2. Identify several examples of participant observation (from the references or journals listed in the Chapter 1 exercises). Specify the methods used for analyzing data and generalizing. What were the strengths and weaknesses of this approach? Would you do it differently? Why or why not?

3. Identify two examples of participant observation from the literature. What form of analysis and theorizing were employed? Discuss the strengths and weaknesses of the approaches used.

4. Select a topic for participant observation and indicate how you might conduct analysis and theorizing. Do you favor a particular style of theorizing? Why or why not?

9

Leaving the Field and Communicating Results

Leaving the field and writing up findings, the last phases of participant observation, are discussed in this chapter. Different experiences of departing the field setting are described and illustrated. Suggestions and strategies for communicating findings are presented.

LEAVING THE EVERYDAY LIFE SETTING

Departure from the everyday life setting of participant observation commonly is a routine process. As you move from concentrating on the collection of data and making notes to establishing files, analyzing findings, and theorizing, the amount of time spent in the field generally decreases. Withdrawal from the field comes about in a number of different ways (see Maines et al., 1980). The objectives of study, for instance, may have been satisfied (see Spradley, 1970; Fine, 1987).

A finite period of field study may be planned from the outset, due to the availability of resources and/or deadlines. Depending on what transpires, field study might be renegotiated for longer or shorter periods of time. This situation is common, for instance, in evaluation research and projects supported by external funding. Hebert (1986) completed the evaluation of two innovative programs in Native American education. Manning's (1977, 1980) fieldwork with British police was limited partly by external funding. Jules-Rosette's (1975) fieldwork in Africa also was limited by the resources available for supporting research in a distant place.

At the outset, the participant observer may be committed to remaining in the field for whatever length of time is necessary. I had no definite preconception, for instance, of the length of time to be spent studying American occultism. While I hoped to complete a doctoral dissertation, such a project runs three, four, five years, or longer. In some cases, the topic of field study is or becomes a lifetime preoccupation of the researcher. This may lead to periodic efforts to collect subsequent data (see Mead, 1923). It may be difficult to end relationships with people, whether or not further research is planned, especially when close and intimate friendships have been established and sustained over lengthy periods (see Maines et al., 1980; Roadburg, 1980; Snow, 1980).

Unanticipated, intervening factors may influence, even dictate, the termination of study. For a variety of reasons, such as personal health, safety, motivation, and relationships, the participant observer may decide to end research. Or events within the everyday life setting, such as changes in people and objects of study, conflicts among individuals or groups, the development of poor relationships, lack of rapport, being shut out or having permission to observe revoked, may result in a decision to stop inquiry. Although I gradually withdrew from field involvements with occultists, a final ending was dictated when I took a university position in a different state. Political developments in Africa influenced Jules-Rosette's (1975) departure from the field. In most instances, there are a variety of complex reasons for the decision to leave the field (see Altheide, 1980).

Even after leaving the field, participant observers may return periodically to visit friends, or even conduct further research. Manning (1977, 1980) and Jules-Rosette (1975, 1984) have conducted field research over extended periods of time, sometimes on the same or similar topics and sometimes on related but quite different matters. I have maintained periodic contact with close friends and informants in the esoteric community but have not conducted further research in this setting for many years. Whyte (1955, 1984) reports contacts with street-corner society over many years. Damrell (1978) maintained intermittent contact with members of a religious group he studied over many years. His involvements with this group later resulted in participant observation with a different religious group (see Damrell, 1977). His report findings provides no indication that participation with this group ended with the publication of this book.

Leaving the field is an emotional experience. Length and degree of participant involvement intensifies these feelings. Leaving may be experienced as a relief: Fieldwork is difficult, demanding, and emotionally draining, even when it is a mostly pleasant experience, and the researcher commonly anticipates a challenge in writing up and communicating findings. Departure from the field may be a great relief, particularly if fieldwork has been unpleasant. Participant observers sometimes come to detest certain aspects of fieldwork and/or loathe, even hate, specific people or situations. Unless these feelings can be managed, withdrawal is imperative. Your experience in departing the field commonly will range from joy and relief to regret and even sadness.

There rarely is an ideal time or way of withdrawing from the field. There are questions still in need of answers, bits and pieces of unfinished business, matters that might be explored. Commonly there are people, including friends, who will be missed. It is appropriate to leave the field once you have addressed the basic study questions and issues. Withdrawal is best managed over a period of time so that everyone is able to prepare for the end of participant observational study. You eventually will spend greater portions of time and energy on notes and files and significantly less time on sustaining field relationships and collecting data. In many cases, this transition is gradual and occurs as part of the natural course of working through analysis and report writing.

COMMUNICATING FINDINGS

Writing up findings may begin in the field, but it generally continues, oftentimes with increased urgency and productivity, once you leave the field. Writing may continue for several years. Disengagement from the setting of study is necessary to gain sufficient time and distance from the problem studied to communicate results effectively (see Altheide, 1980).

The Writing Process

What you say about research findings depends on the audience or audiences to be addressed. Writing is rhetoric; it seeks to convince, persuade, argue, and demonstrate. A naive audience, such as the general public, requires you to spell out carefully even the most obvious points, avoid technical jargon, and employ ordinary language. Audiences of professional peers may require you to address only the most salient, central facts, leaving much of the commonsense and even theoretical context implicit. Many times you are not at all certain of the audience. The task of writing is much easier when you anticipate, imaginatively if necessary, the people with whom you intend to communicate.

Writing is a form of thinking, not simply a mechanical process of presenting results. There are, consequently, many different styles of writing and no absolutely "right" way. Initially, you should try simply to write up results of research and not worry about how you are writing. Little can be done with your writing until your ideas have been committed to written words.

Unfortunately, many people see writing as a magical ritual (Becker, 1986). They want to know the secrets to getting ideas written down and transforming a rough draft into a polished copy. What these people do not understand, according to Becker, is that no writer ever gets things correct or perfect the first time, or even the second or perhaps the third time. Early drafts should be understood as an expression of potentially relevant ideas. The order, logic, and organization of this expression remains to be discovered through further work and subsequent drafts. Multiple drafts are not only normal, they are required. Writing is doing, not wishing.

Writing is a process. It begins by expressing research results in verbal form. For the participant observer, this is accomplished through the construction of notes and files. A next step is to construct a draft on a topic, issue, or problem to be communicated to an audience. Early drafts are not unlike thinking aloud in that they are more suggestive than definite. How particular ideas might be arranged with respect to one another, in what sequence, and in terms of what patterns, perspectives, models, or theories is what you are exploring. Preliminary drafts will lead to other ideas and suggest possible connections among these concepts. Subsequent drafts build on this foundation, developing the ideas further, especially the order or logic of the presentation. No draft or version is ever complete in any absolute sense. There always are other ways of expressing and arranging some set of ideas. A draft, therefore, is finished when you decide that it communicates what you intend and you are unable or unwilling to work on it further.

Although there is not one correct method of writing, it is possible to suggest useful guidelines. So long as the participant observer understands that writing is a continuation of processes of making notes, analyzing, and generalizing findings, getting started should not be a problem. Through these activities, you already have made progress toward writing up findings.

Outlines may be very helpful once you have notes and files in need of further organization. Outlines, however, are purely heuristic devices. You need an outline only to get a handle on the possible arrangement of ideas or an argument. The outline serves temporarily to organize your thinking and provide a definitive direction to the work. Be prepared to deviate from your outline. The outline should stimulate you to develop ideas and uncover connections among facts you have not anticipated up to this point. The usefulness of a good outline is quickly exhausted in that, if it is a good outline, it leads to new and different possibilities not yet considered. Once you have a draft of an argument, it may be helpful to outline it. Such an outline may clarify your thinking, highlight the (only implicit) logic, and suggest missing pieces or alternative arrangements of ideas. As you move through subsequent drafts, the process of writing, outlining, and writing may be repeated fruitfully.

Editing will improve the effectiveness of the ideas communicated by a draft. It may be the most important aspect of writing. Editing involves reworking what you have written with an eye toward making it communicate better—more effectively, more clearly—to your intended audience. In editing you may be able to eliminate much of what you have written. Do remove words or phrases you are able to eliminate without changing the basic content or meaning of the communication. Break up compound sentences into shorter, more precise expressions. Use concise, succinct sentences whenever possible.

There are a number of other basic recommendations for constructing clear and effective written communications. Becker (1986), for instance, suggests the following principles:

—Use active rather than passive verbs when possible. Active verbs force you to identify what you are talking about with some specificity.
—Avoid the use of two or more words when one will do. Eliminate unnecessary words when editing.
—Ordinary words generally communicate better than unusual or even highly technical expressions. Even with professional audiences, a little jargon goes a long way.
—Avoid repetition. It is best to say exactly what you mean as concisely as possible in the first place.
—Be concrete and specific rather than abstract and general whenever possible.
—Use examples and illustrations to fill out the meaning of basic ideas. Examples and illustrations are especially important in presenting participant observational findings. They also are extremely helpful in communicating abstract concepts and principles.
—Be careful of metaphors: Use metaphors seriously, not carelessly.

Reporting Participant Observational Findings

Because every project is to some extent unique, no specific outline or form for reporting the results of participant observation will be appropriate for every study. It may be helpful, nevertheless, to suggest a general outline of topics you may wish to consider in developing your participant observational report.

(1) It is helpful to state as concisely as possible the basic problem you intend to address in the report. Discuss perspectives, models, theories, and literature relevant to this topic/problem. The focus of the research, as defined by key ideas and conceptions, should be identified and discussed.

(2) Discuss research methods and strategies. Talk about the setting, gaining entry, and procedures for establishing rapport and sustaining relations. Describe strategies and procedures related to the participant role, data collection, analysis, and theorizing.

(3) Discuss the major findings of research. Precisely what this involves depends on the study problem and issues to be addressed, as well as the information you collected.

(4) Discuss the significance of the findings or what they represent. What can be concluded from your participant observational study?

Do not agonize over omitting particular facts or even larger portions of findings. Much of the data may not be useful for a given report. Large portions of field data may never find their way into written reports. Participant observers commonly find it necessary or desirable to include material difficult to integrate into the body of the report by way of an appendix, preface, epilogue, or afterword, or even as a lengthy substantive note. Digressions sometimes turn up as separate chapters, articles, or reports related to the central problem and issues but inappropriate for inclusion in the original report.

It is useful to begin with the body of the report: the chapters or sections dealing with the major findings. Then attention may be focused on related issues. There is no need for an introduction, for instance, until you have something to introduce. It is difficult to discuss methods of data collection or relevant literature until the findings have been reviewed.

I find it most productive to write up the basic results, having a fairly specific definition of the problem in mind. I then revise my problem statement in terms of the draft of the findings, and continue to work over these sections until I feel the basic issues have been addressed adequately. Next, I write a summary and concluding section. I use this to draft an introduction. From the introduction, I work through each of the subsequent sections of the report. Then I rewrite the summary and conclusions. If all goes well, this rough draft may be honed and polished until I have a report appropriate for communicating to a professional audience, and perhaps eventually for publication.

SUMMARY

There is no absolute end to participant observational research in most cases. Participant observers sometimes are forced or decide to leave a setting, but departure from the field commonly comes about as a routine process of moving from the collection of data and making notes and files to analyzing, generalizing, theorizing, and writing preliminary reports of findings. There are a wide variety of *feelings* associated with leaving the field. The participant observer and people in the setting may experience relief, joy, regret, loss, and sadness. It may be possible to anticipate departure from the field, negotiating and managing its consequences for yourself and other people.

Writing is a form of thinking. It is a continuation of the process of analysis and theorizing. There is nothing especially magical about it. Writing is facilitated by blocks of uninterrupted time. It is helpful to anticipate the audience or audiences with whom you intend to communicate. Writing is a process that involves drafting and redrafting reports of findings. Eventually, a report is produced. This chapter contains a variety of general recommendations for writing and specific suggestions for communicating the results of participant observations.

EXERCISES

1. Select an article reporting the results of participant observational research from the literature. Edit this article on the basis of the suggestions offered in this chapter. What kinds of changes were you able to make in the text? Did these changes improve the text? Explain your answer.
2. Generate an outline of some set of participant observational findings you produced by way of this book. Construct a draft of your findings on the basis of this outline. Indicate how the outline helped to organize your thinking. Also indicate how you were able to move beyond the outline in writing up your results.
3. Select a report of participant observation research and an example of a report of some other method of human study from the literature. Compare and contrast these reports, discussing basic similarities and differences. To what extent are the differences a reflection of the different methods of study?
4. Examine the literature on participant observation for reports of experiences in leaving the field. Select several reports of withdrawal from the field and briefly compare and contrast them.

REFERENCES

Adler, P. 1981. *Momentum*. Beverly Hills, CA: Sage.
———— and P. A. Adler. 1987. *Membership Roles in Field Research*. Beverly Hills, CA: Sage.
Adler, P. A. 1985. *Wheeling and Dealing*. New York: Columbia University Press.
Adler, P. A., P. Adler, and E. B. Rochford, Jr., eds. 1986. "The Politics of Participation in Field Research" [Special issue]. *Urban Life* 14(4, January).
Agar, M. H. 1986a. *Independents Declared*. Washington, DC: Smithsonian Institution Press.
————. 1986b. *Speaking of Ethnography*. Beverly Hills, CA: Sage.
Altheide, D. L. 1976. *Creating Reality*. Beverly Hills, CA: Sage.
————. 1980. "Leaving the Newsroom." Pp. 301-10 in *Fieldwork Experience*, edited by W. B. Shaffir et al. New York: St. Martin.
————. 1985. *Media Power*. Beverly Hills, CA: Sage.
————. 1987. "Ethnographic Content Analysis." *Qualitative Sociology* 10(1):65-77.
———— and J. M. Johnson. 1977. "Counting Souls." *Pacific Sociological Review* (July):328-48.
Altheide, D. L. and R. Snow. 1979. *Media Logic*. Beverly Hills, CA: Sage.
Anderson, E. 1978. *A Place on the Corner*. Chicago: University of Chicago Press.
Angell, R. C. 1936. *The Family Encounters the Depression*. New York: Scribner.
Babbie, E. 1973. *Survey Research Methods*. Belmont, CA: Wadsworth.
————. 1986. *The Practice of Social Research*. Belmont, CA: Wadsworth.
Bateson, G. and M. Mead. 1942. *Balinese Character*. New York: Academy of Sciences.
Becker, H. S. 1963. *Outsiders*. New York: Free Press.
————. 1968. "Social Observation and Social Case Studies." Pp. 232-38 in *International Encyclopedia of the Social Sciences*, edited by D. L. Sills. New York: Macmillan.
————. 1969. "Problems of Inference and Proof in Participant Observation." Pp. 260-76 in *Issues in Participant Observation*, edited by G. J. McCall and J. L. Simmons. Reading, MA: Addison-Wesley.
————, ed. 1981. *Exploring Society Photographically*. Chicago: University of Chicago Press.
————. 1986. *Writing for Social Scientists*. Chicago: University of Chicago Press.
————, B. Greer, E. C. Hughes, and A. L. Strauss. 1961. *Boys in White: Student Culture in Medical School*. Chicago: University of Chicago Press.
Bellman, B. L. 1984. *The Language of Secrecy*. New Brunswick, NJ: Rutgers University Press.
———— and B. Jules-Rosette. 1977. *A Paradigm for Looking*. Norwood, NJ: Ablex.
Berger, B. M. 1981. *The Survival of a Counterculture*. Berkeley: University of California Press.
Berger, P. L. and T. Luckmann. 1966. *The Social Construction of Reality*. New York: Doubleday.
Bertaux, D., ed. 1981. *Biography and Society*. Beverly Hills, CA: Sage.
Birdwhistell, R. L. 1952. *Introduction to Kinesics*. Louisville, KY: University of Louisville Press.

Blalock, H. M., Jr. 1971. *Causal Models in the Social Sciences.* Chicago: Aldine & Atherton.

Blau, P. 1964. "The Research Process in the Study of *The Dynamics of Bureaucracy.*" Pp. 16-49 in *Sociologists at Work*, edited by P. E. Hammond. New York: Basic Books.

Blumer, H. 1954. "What Is Wrong with Social Theory?" *American Sociological Review* 19:3-10.

———. 1969. *Symbolic Interactionism.* Englewood Cliffs, NJ: Prentice-Hall.

Broadhead, R. S. 1983. *The Private Lives and Professional Identity of Medical Students.* New Brunswick, NJ: Transaction.

Bromley, D. G. and A. D. Shupe, Jr. 1979. *"Moonies" in America.* Beverly Hills, CA: Sage.

Bruyn, S. T. 1966. *The Human Perspective in Sociology.* Englewood Cliffs, NJ: Prentice-Hall.

Bulmer, M., ed. 1982. *Social Research Ethics.* London: Macmillan.

Cassell, J. and M. L. Wax, eds. 1980. "Ethical Problems of Fieldwork" [Special issue]. *Social Problems* 27(February).

Chenitz, W. C. and J. M. Swanson, eds. 1986. *From Practice to Grounded Theory.* Menlo Park, CA: Addison-Wesley.

Cicourel, A. V. 1964. *Method and Measurement in Sociology.* New York: Free Press.

———. 1968. *The Social Organization of Juvenile Justice.* New York: John Wiley.

———. 1974. *Theory and Method in a Study of Argentine Fertility.* New York: John Wiley.

Clandinin, D. J. 1985. "Personal Practical Knowledge." *Curriculum Inquiry* 15(4):361-85.

Clifford, J. and G. E. Marcus, eds. 1986. *Writing Culture.* Berkeley: University of California Press.

Collier, J., Jr. 1967. *Visual Anthropology.* New York: Holt, Rinehart & Winston.

Conrad, P. and S. Reinhartz, eds. 1984. "Computers and Qualitative Data" [Special issue]. *Qualitative Sociology* 7(2, Spring/Summer).

Cook, T. D. and E. T. Campbell. 1979. *Quasi-Experimentation.* Chicago: Rand McNally.

Cooley, C. H. 1902. *Human Nature and the Social Order.* New York: Scribner.

———. 1909. *Social Organization.* New York: Scribner.

———. 1918. *The Social Process.* New York: Scribner.

———. 1969. *Sociological Theory and Social Research.* New York: A. M. Kelley. [Original work published 1930]

Corsaro, W. A. 1985. *Friendship and Peer Culture in the Early Years.* Norwood, NJ: Ablex.

Cottle, T. J. 1977. *Private Lives and Public Accounts.* Amherst: University of Massachusetts Press.

Cressey, D. R. 1953. *Other People's Money.* New York: Free Press.

Dalton, M. 1959. *Men Who Manage.* New York: John Wiley.

———. 1964. "Preconception and Methods in *Men Who Manage.*" Pp. 50-95 in *Sociologists at Work*, edited by P. E. Hammond. New York: Basic Books.

Damrell, J. 1977. *Seeking Spiritual Meaning.* Beverly Hills, CA: Sage.

———. 1978. *Search for Identity.* Beverly Hills, CA: Sage.

Delph, E. W. 1978. *The Silent Community.* Beverly Hills, CA: Sage.

Denzin, N. K. 1978. *The Research Act.* New York: McGraw-Hill.

———. Forthcoming. "Review Symposium on Field Methods." *Journal of Contemporary Ethnography.*

Dollard, J. 1937. *Caste and Class in a Southern Town.* New Haven, CT: Yale University Press.

Douglas, J. D. 1976. *Investigative Social Research*. Beverly Hills, CA: Sage.

———. 1985. *Creative Interviewing*. Newbury Park, CA: Sage.

———, P. A. Adler, P. Adler, A. Fontana, Freeman, and J. A. Kotarba. 1980. *Introduction to the Sociologies of Everyday Life*. Boston: Allyn & Bacon.

Douglas, J. D. and J. M. Johnson, eds. 1977. *Existential Sociology*. New York: Cambridge University Press.

Douglas, J. D. and P. K. Rasmussen, with C. A. Flanagan. 1977. *The Nude Beach*. Beverly Hills, CA: Sage.

Dressler, W. W. 1987. "The Stress Process in a Southern Black Community." *Human Organization* 46(3):211-20.

Easterday, L., D. Papodemas, L. Shorr, and C. Valentini. 1977. "The Making of a Female Researcher." *Urban Life* 6:333-48.

Easthope, G. 1971. *A History of Social Research Methods*. New York: Longman.

Ellis, C. 1986. *Fisher Folk*. Lexington: University of Kentucky Press.

Emerson, R. M. 1969. *Judging Delinquents*. Chicago: Aldine.

———, ed. 1983. *Contemporary Field Research*. Boston: Little, Brown.

Feldman, H. W., M. H. Agar, and G. M. Beschner. 1979. *Angel Dust*. Lexington, MA: Lexington Books.

Ferraro, K. J. 1981. "Battered Women and the Shelter Movement." Ph.D. dissertation, Arizona State University, Tempe, Department of Sociology.

Festinger, L., H. W. Riecken, and S. Schacter. 1956. *When Prophecy Fails*. Minneapolis: University of Minnesota Press.

Fine, G. A. 1987. *With the Boys*. Chicago: University of Chicago Press.

Fischer, P. J. 1979. "Precocious Pregnancies." Ph.D. dissertation, University of Florida, Gainesville, Department of Anthropology.

Forrest, B. 1986. "Apprentice-Participation." *Urban Life* 14:431-53.

Fowler, F. L., Jr. 1984. *Survey Research Methods*. Beverly Hills, CA: Sage.

Fox, K. J. 1987. "Real Punks and Pretenders." *Journal of Contemporary Ethnography* 16(3):344-70.

Freudenburg, W. R. 1986. "Sociology in Legis-Land." *Sociological Quarterly* 27(3):313-24.

Gallimeier, C. P. 1987. "Putting on the Game Face." *Sociology of Sport Journal* 4:347-62.

———. Forthcoming. *Twenty Minutes to Broadway*. Philadelphia, PA: Temple University Press.

Gans, H. J. 1962. *The Urban Villagers*. New York: Free Press.

Garfinkel, H. 1967. *Studies in Ethnomethodology*. Englewood Cliffs, NJ: Prentice-Hall.

Geertz, C. 1973. *The Interpretation of Cultures*. New York: Basic Books.

Gibbs, J. P. 1972. *Sociological Theory Construction*. Hillsdale, IL: Dryden.

Glazer, B. C. and A. L. Strauss. 1967. *The Discovery of Grounded Theory*. Chicago: Aldine.

Goffman, E. 1959. *The Presentation of Self in Everyday Life*. Garden City, NY: Doubleday.

———. 1961. *Asylums*. Garden City, NY: Doubleday.

———. 1974. *Frame Analysis*. New York: Harper & Row.

Gold, R. L. 1954. "Toward a Social Interaction Methodology for Sociological Field Observation." Ph.D. dissertation, University of Chicago, Department of Sociology.

———. 1958. "Roles in Sociological Field Observations." *Social Forces* 36:217-23.

———. 1969. "Roles in Sociological Field Observations," Pp. 30-39 in *Issues in Participant Observation*, edited by G. J. McCall and J. L. Simmons. Reading MA: Addison-Wesley.

Golde, P., ed. 1970. *Women in the Field*. Chicago: Aldine.

Gordon, D. F. 1987. "Getting Close by Staying Distant." *Qualitative Sociology* 10(3):267-87.

Haaken, J. and R. Adams. 1983. "Pathology as 'Personal Growth.'" *Psychiatry* 46(3):270-80.

Hall, E. T. 1959. *The Silent Language*. New York: Anchor.

———. 1966. *The Hidden Dimension*. New York: Anchor.

———. 1976. *Beyond Culture*. New York: Anchor.

Hammersley, M. and P. Atkinson. 1983. *Ethnography*. London: Tavistock.

Hayano, D. H. 1982. *Poker Faces*. Berkeley: University of California Press.

Hebert, Y. M. 1986. "Naturalistic Evaluation in Practice." *Curriculum Inquiry* 15(4):361-85.

Hilbert, R. A. 1980. "Covert Participant Observation." *Urban Life* 9:51-78.

Hinkle, R. C. and G. J. Hinkle. 1954. *The Development of Modern Sociology*. New York: Random House.

Hochschild, A. R. 1983. *The Managed Heart*. Berkeley: University of California Press.

Hockey, J. 1986. *Squaddies*. Ester: Wheaton.

Hocking, P., ed. 1975. *Principles of Visual Anthropology*. The Hague, the Netherlands: Mouton.

Horowitz, R. 1983. *Honor and the American Dream*. New Brunswick, NJ: Rutgers University Press.

Hughes, P. H. 1977. *Behind the Wall of Respect*. Chicago: University of Chicago Press.

Humphreys, L. 1970. *Tea-Room Trade*. Chicago: Aldine.

Hunt, J. 1984. "The Development of Rapport Through the Negotiation of Gender in Field Work Among Police." *Human Organization* 43(4):283-95.

Husband, R. L. 1985. "Toward a Grounded Typology of Organizational Leadership Behavior." *Quarterly Journal of Speech* 71:103-18.

Irwin, J. 1970. *The Felon*. Englewood Cliffs, NJ: Prentice-Hall.

———. 1980. *Prisons in Turmoil*. Boston: Little, Brown.

Jacobs, J. 1977. *Stateville*. Chicago: University of Chicago Press.

Johnson, J. M. 1975. *Doing Field Research*. New York: Free Press.

———. 1977. "Behind the Rational Appearances." Pp. 201-228 in *Existential Sociology*, edited by J. D. Douglas and J. M. Johnson. Cambridge: Cambridge University Press.

Jorgensen, D. L. 1979. "Tarot Divination in the Valley of the Sun." Ph.D. dissertation, Ohio State University, Columbus, Department of Sociology.

———. 1982. "The Esoteric Community: An Ethnographic Investigation of the Cultic Milieu." *Urban Life* 10(4):383-407.

———. 1983. "Psychic Fairs: A Basis of Solidarity and Networks Among Occultists." *California Sociologist* 6(1):57-75.

———. 1984. "Divinatory Discourse." *Symbolic Interaction* 7(2, Summer/Fall): 135-53.

——— and L. Jorgensen. 1982. "Social Meanings of the Occult." *Sociological Quarterly* 23(3, Summer):373-89.

Jules-Rosette, B. 1975. *African Apostles*. Ithaca, NY: Cornell University Press.

———. 1984. *The Messages of Tourist Art*. New York: Plenum.

Junker, B. H. 1960. *Field Work*. Chicago: University of Chicago Press.

Kaplan, A. 1964. *The Conduct of Inquiry*. San Francisco: Chandler.

Kirk, J. and M. L. Miller. 1986. *Reliability and Validity in Qualitative Research*. Beverly Hills, CA: Sage.

Kirk, R. C. 1981. "Microcomputers in Anthropological Research." Pp. 473-92 in

Microcomputers in Social Research, edited by D. R. Heise. Beverly Hills, CA: Sage.

Kleinman, S. 1984. *Equals Before God*. Chicago: University of Chicago Press.

Klockars, C. B. 1974. *The Professional Fence*. New York: Free Press.

————— and F. W. O'Connor, eds. 1979. *Deviance and Decency*. Beverly Hills, CA: Sage.

Knorr-Cetina, K. D. and M. Mulkay. 1983. *Science Observed*. Beverly Hills, CA: Sage.

Kornblum, N. 1974. *Blue Collar Community*. Chicago: University of Chicago Press.

Kotarba, J. A. 1977. "The Chronic Pain Experience." Pp. 257-72 in *Existential Sociology*, edited by J. P. Douglas and J. M. Johnson. Cambridge: Cambridge University Press.

—————. 1980. "Discovering Amorphous Social Experience." Pp. 57-67 in *Fieldwork Experience*, edited by W. B. Shaffir et al. New York: St. Martin.

—————. 1983. *Chronic Pain*. Beverly Hills, CA: Sage.

————— and A. Fontana, eds. 1984. *The Existential Self in Society*. Chicago: University of Chicago Press.

Krieger, S. 1985. "Beyond Subjectivity." *Qualitative Sociology* 8:309-24.

Kuhn, T. 1970. *The Structure of Scientific Revolutions*. Chicago: University of Chicago Press.

Latour, B. and S. Woolgar. 1979. *Laboratory Life*. Beverly Hills, CA: Sage.

Lazarsfeld, P. F. 1972. *Qualitative Analysis*. Boston: Allyn & Bacon.

Liebow, E. 1967. *Tally's Corner*. Boston: Little, Brown.

Lindeman, E. C. 1923. *Social Discovery*. New York: Republic Press.

Lindesmith, A. R. 1947. *Opiate Addiction*. Bloomington, IL: Principa.

Lofland, J. 1966. *Doomsday Cult*. Englewood Cliffs, NJ: Prentice-Hall.

—————. 1971. *Analyzing Social Settings*. Belmont, CA: Wadsworth.

————— and L. H. Lofland. 1984. *Analyzing Social Settings*. Belmont, CA: Wadsworth.

Lyman, S. M. and M. B. Scott. 1970. *A Sociology of the Absurd*. New York: Appleton-Century-Crofts.

—————. 1975. *The Drama of Social Reality*. New York: Oxford.

Lynch, M. 1985. *Art and Artifact in Laboratory Science*. London: Routledge & Kegan Paul.

Lynd, R. S. and H. M. Lynd. 1929. *Middletown*. New York: Harcourt Brace.

MacIver, R. M. 1942. *Social Causation*. Boston: Ginn.

Maines, D. R., W. Shaffir, and A. Turowetz. 1980. "Leaving the Field in Ethnographic Research." Pp. 261-80 in *Fieldwork Experience*, edited by W. B. Shaffir et al. New York: St. Martin.

Mandell, N. 1988. "The Least-Adult Role in Studying Children." *Journal of Contemporary Ethnography* 16(4):433-67.

Manning, P. K. 1977. *Police Work*. Cambridge: MIT Press.

—————. 1980. *The Narcs' Game*. Cambridge, MA: MIT Press.

Masayuki Hamabata, M. 1986. "Ethnographic Boundaries." *Qualitative Sociology* 9(4):354-71.

McCall, G. J. 1978. *Observing the Law*. New York: Free Press.

————— and J. L. Simmons. 1969. *Issues in Participant Observation*. Reading, MA: Addison-Wesley.

Mead, M. 1923. *Coming of Age in Samoa*. New York: William Morrow.

Mehan, H. 1974. "Accomplishing Classroom Lessons." Pp. 76-142 in *Language Use and School Performance*, edited by A. V. Cicourel et al. New York: Academic Press.

————— and H. Wood. 1975. *The Reality of Ethnomethodology*. New York: John Wiley.

Miller, E. M. 1986. *Street Women*. Philadelphia: Temple University Press.

Milner, C. and R. Milner. 1972. *Black Players*. Boston: Little, Brown.

Mitchell, R. G., Jr. 1983. *Mountain Experience*. Chicago: University of Chicago Press.

Molstad, C. 1986. "Choosing and Coping with Boring Work." *Urban Life* 15(2):215-36.

Palmer, V. 1928. *Field Studies in Sociology.* Chicago: University of Chicago Press.

Pastner, C. 1982. "Rethinking the Role of the Woman Field Worker in Purdah Societies." *Human Organization* 41:262-64.

Peshkin, A. 1986. *God's Choice.* Chicago: University of Chicago Press.

Polkinghorne, D. 1983. *Methodology for the Human Sciences.* Albany: State University of New York Press.

Polsky, N. 1969. *Hustlers, Beats and Others.* New York: Anchor.

Ponse, B. 1976. "Secrecy in the Lesbian World." *Urban Life* 5:313-38.

Preble, E. and J. J. Casey, Jr. 1969. "Taking Care of Business." *International Journal of the Addictions* 4(1):1-24.

Preble, E. and T. Miller. 1977. "Methadone, Wine, and Welfare." Pp. 229-48 in *Street Ethnography*, edited by R. S. Weppner. Beverly Hills, CA: Sage.

Psathas, G., ed. 1973. *Phenomenological Sociology.* New York: John Wiley.

Punch, M. 1986. *The Politics and Ethics of Fieldwork.* Beverly Hills, CA: Sage.

Rabinow, P. 1977. *Reflections on Fieldwork in Morocco.* Berkeley: University of California Press.

Rambo, C. A. 1987. "Turn-Ons for Money." M.A. thesis, University of South Florida, Tampa, Department of Sociology.

Reimer, J. W. 1977. "Varieties of Opportunistic Research." *Urban Life* 5:467-77.

Richard, M. P. 1986. "Goffman Revisited." *Qualitative Sociology* 9(4):321-38.

Roadburg, A. 1980. "Breaking Relationships with Research Subjects." Pp. 281-91 in *Fieldwork Experience*, edited by W. B. Shaffir et al. New York: St. Martin.

Roethlisberger, F. J. and W. J. Dickson. 1939. *Management and the Worker.* Cambridge, MA: Harvard University Press.

Sanders, C. R. 1988. "Marks of Mischief." *Journal of Contemporary Ethnography* 16(4):433-67.

Schatzman, L. and A. L. Strauss. 1973. *Field Research.* Englewood Cliffs, NJ: Prentice-Hall.

Schrodt, P. A. 1984. *Microcomputer Methods for Social Scientists.* Beverly Hills, CA: Sage.

Schutz, A. 1967. *The Phenomenology of the Social World.* Chicago: University of Chicago Press.

Scott, M. 1968. *The Racing Game.* Chicago: Aldine.

Shaffir, W. B., R. A. Stebbins, and A. Turowetz. 1980. *Fieldwork Experience.* New York: St. Martin.

Shupe, J. 1970. *The Felon.* Englewood Cliffs, NJ: Prentice-Hall.

——— and D. G. Bromley. 1980. *The Vigilantes.* Beverly Hills, CA: Sage.

Simmel, G. 1950. *The Sociology of George Simmel*, translated by K. H. Wolff. New York: Free Press.

Snow, D. A. 1980. "The Disengagement Process." *Qualitative Sociology* 3:100-22.

Spradley, J. 1970. *You Owe Yourself a Drunk.* Boston: Little, Brown.

———. 1979. *The Ethnographic Interview.* New York: Holt, Rinehart & Winston.

———. 1980. *Participant Observation.* New York: Holt, Rinehart & Winston.

Strauss, A. 1987. *Qualitative Analysis for Social Scientists.* Cambridge: Cambridge University Press.

Sudnow, D. 1967. *Passing On.* Englewood Cliffs, NJ: Prentice-Hall.

———. 1978. *Ways of the Hand.* Cambridge, MA: Harvard University Press.

Sutherland, E. and C. Conwell. 1967. *Professional Thief.* Chicago: University of Chicago Press.

Suttles, G. D. 1968. *The Social Order of the Slum*. Chicago: University of Chicago Press.
———. 1972. *The Social Construction of Communities*. Chicago: University of Chicago Press.
Taylor, S. J. 1987. "Observing Abuse." *Qualitative Sociology* 10(3):288-302.
Thomas, J. 1983. "Toward a Critical Ethnography." *Urban Life* 11:477-90.
Thomas, W. I. and D. S. Thomas. 1928. *The Child in America*. New York: Knopf.
Thomas, W. I. and F. Znaniecki. 1918-19. *The Polish Peasant in Europe and America*. Chicago: University of Chicago Press.
Unruh, D. R. 1983. *Invisible Lives*. Beverly Hills, CA: Sage.
Van Maanen, J., ed. 1983. *Qualitative Methodology*. Beverly Hills, CA: Sage.
Vesperi, M. D. 1985. *City of Green Benches*. Ithaca, NY: Cornell University Press.
Vidich, A. J. and J. Bensman. 1968. *Small Town in Mass Society*. Princeton, NJ: Princeton University Press.
Wallace, W. 1971. *The Logic of Science in Sociology*. Chicago: Aldine.
Wallis, R. 1977. *The Road to Total Freedom*. New York: Columbia University Press.
Warner, W. L. 1959. *The Living and the Dead: A Study of the Symbolism of Americans*. New Haven, CT: Yale University Press.
Warner, W. L. and P. Lunt. 1941. *The Social Life of a Modern Community*. New Haven, CT: Yale University Press.
———. 1942. *The Status System of a Modern Society*. New Haven, CT: Yale University Press.
Warner, W. L. and L. Srole. 1945. *The Social Systems of American Ethnic Groups*. Vol. 3, *Yankee City*. New Haven, CT: Yale University Press.
Warren, C.A.B. 1974. *Identity and Community in the Gay World*. New York: John Wiley.
——— and P. K. Rasmussen. 1977. "Sex and Gender in Field Research." *Urban Life* 6:349-69.
Watson, J. D. 1968. *The Double Helix*. New York: Athaneum.
Wax, R. H. 1971. *Doing Fieldwork*. Chicago: University of Chicago Press.
———. 1979. "Gender and Age in Fieldwork and Fieldwork Education." *Social Problems* 26:509-22.
Webb, S. and B. Webb. 1932. *Methods of Social Study*. New York: Longman, Green.
Weber, M. 1949. *The Methodology of the Social Sciences*. Glencoe, IL: Free Press.
Weppner, R. S. 1983. *The Untherapeutic Community*. Lincoln: University of Nebraska Press.
Whyte, W. F. 1955. *Street Corner Society*. Chicago: University of Chicago Press.
———. 1984. *Learning from the Field*. Beverly Hills, CA: Sage.
Wiley, J. 1987. "The 'Shock of Unrecognition' as a Problem in Participant-Observation." *Qualitative Sociology* 10(1):78-83.
Williams, D. D., ed. 1986. *Naturalistic Evaluation*. San Francisco: Jossey-Bass.
Wiseman, J. P. 1970. *Stations of the Lost*. Englewood Cliffs, NJ: Prentice-Hall.
Woods, P. 1985. "Sociology, Ethnography and Teacher Practice." *Teaching and Teacher Education* 1(1):51-62.
Wright, S. 1978. *Crowds and Riots*. Beverly Hills, CA: Sage.
Yin, R. K. 1984. *Case Study Research*. Beverly Hills, CA: Sage.
Zimmerman, D. H. and D. L. Weider. 1977. "The Diary." *Urban Life* 5(4):479-98.
Znaniecki, F. 1935. *The Method of Sociology*. New York: Holt, Rinehart & Winston.
———. 1952. *Cultural Sciences*. Urbana: University of Illinois Press.
———. 1965. *Social Relations and Social Roles*. San Francisco: Chandler.
Zurcher, L. A. 1977. *The Mutable Self*. Beverly Hills, CA: Sage.

INDEX

ABOUT THE AUTHOR

Danny L. Jorgensen is Associate Professor of Sociology with the Center for Interdisciplinary Studies in Culture and Society at the University of South Florida, St. Petersburg. He holds a Ph.D. from Ohio State University, an M.A. from Western Kentucky University, and a B.S. from Northern Arizona University. His participant observational research on new and socially marginal religious movements has appeared in the *American Journal of Sociology, Sociological Quarterly, Urban Life* (now the *Journal of Contemporary Ethnography*), and *Symbolic Interactionism*. Currently he is engaged in participant observational studies of Vietnam veterans and their families and of Mormon splinter groups.

NOTES